THE SCHOOL OF JOURNALISM

THE SCHOOL OF JOURNALISM IN COLUMBIA UNIVERSITY

THE BOOK THAT TRANSFORMED JOURNALISM FROM A TRADE INTO A PROFESSION

BY

JOSEPH PULITZER

FOUNDER OF THE PULITZER PRIZE

WITH

"THE SCHOOL OF JOURNALISM" BY HORACE WHITE

THE SCHOOL OF JOURNALISM IN COLUMBIA UNIVERSITY" BY JOSEPH PULITZER

"THE POWER OF PUBLIC OPINION" BY JOSEPH PULITZER

FOREWORD BY MICHAEL W. PERRY

INKLING BOOKS   SEATTLE   2006

Description

This book contains a facsimile reproduction of a 1904 book in which Joseph Pulitzer explained why he wanted to found a school of journalism at Columbia University. It also includes two 1903 newspaper articles on the topic and a 1904 magazine article critical of both 'yellow journalism' and Pulitzer's plan to transform journalism into a profession with a formal, university education.

Copyright Notice

Publisher's Note

"School of Journalism" (page 6) is the title page of a May 1904 article in *North American Review* that was later published as a book by Columbia University and is republished here as that book in facsimile.

"School of Journalism for Columbia University" (pages 8–9) was published on page 1 of Joseph Pulitzer's newspaper, *The World*, on Sunday, August 16, 1903.

"Pulitzer Founds Journalism School" (page 10) appeared on page 1 on the *New York Times* on Sunday, August 16, 1903. Only the first part of that article is reproduced here. The rest repeated material from *The World*.

"The School of Journalism" by Horace White (pages 11–18) was published in *North American Review* in January, 1904, pages 25–32. The author is critical of 'yellow journalism' and Pulitzer's plans for a school of journalism.

"The School of Journalism in Columbia University" (pages 19–68) was Joseph Pulitzer's reply to the Horace White article and first appeared in the May 1904 issue of *North American Review*. It was republished later that year as a book by Columbia University. The book version is included here in facsimile.

"The Power of Public Opinion" (pages 69–81) by Joseph Pulitzer was originally published in *Encyclopedia Americana*. It was republished in the same Columbia University book as the previous article.

In the back of this book (pages 82–111) are sample pages from books by Inkling Books. The first three, *Free Lover*, *Lady Eugenist*, and *The Pivot of Civilization in Historical Perspective*, explore issues of sex, reproduction, and eugenics as debated during the era when Pulitzer was a prominent journalist and publisher. There is a historical parallel between the careers of Joseph Pulitzer and Victoria Woodhull, who is the focus of the first two books. Pulitzer became famous and rich, in part, because he realized that high-speed, steam-driven printing presses could provide inexpensive newspapers for the masses. In a similar fashion, Victoria Woodhull was one the first to realize that the nation's extensive, steam-powered, post-Civil War rail system allowed a talented and controversial speaker to get rich speaking to a thousand or more people in a different city each night. Both illustrate a pattern that continues today, the impact of new technology on public opinion.

Special Thanks

To the Office of Public Affairs at Columbia University and in particular to photographer, Joseph Pineiro, for the photograph of the sculpture of Joseph Pulitzer used on the front cover. The sculpture is displayed in the "World Room" at the Graduate School of Journalism.

To the University of Washington Libraries, whose extensive collection included the printed material reproduced in this book.

Library Cataloging Data

The School of Journalism in Columbia University: The Book that Transformed Journalism from a Trade into a Profession

Joseph Pulitzer (1847–1911) with a Foreword by Michael W. [Wiley] Perry (1948–)

111 pages, Size: 6 x 9 in. or 229 x 152 mm. Thickness: 0.24 in. or 6 mm (paperback)

Library of Congress Control Number: 2006923740   Classification: PN4791.C79   070.7

ISBN-13: 978-1-58742-057-3   ISBN-10: 1-58742-057-0 (alkaline paperback)

ISBN-13: 978-1-58742-058-0   ISBN-10: 1-58742-058-9 (Adobe PDF ebook)

BISAC Subject Headings: BIO025000 BIOGRAPHY & AUTOBIOGRAPHY/Editors, Journalists, Publishers; EDU046000 EDUCATION/Professional Development; HIS036060 HISTORY/United States/20th Century.

Publisher Information

First Inkling Books edition, First Printing, April 2006. Published in the United States of America on acid-free paper. Inkling Books, Seattle, WA, U.S.A. Internet: http://www.InklingBooks.com/

Contents

NORTH AMERICAN REVIEW

No. DLXX.

MAY, 1904.

THE COLLEGE OF JOURNALISM.

A Review of Criticisms and Objections—Reflections Upon the Power, the Progress and the Prejudices of the Press—Why Specialized Concentration and Education at College Would Improve the Character and Work of Journalists and So Promote the Welfare of the Republic.

> *"The man who writes, the man who month in and month out, week in and week out, day in and day out, furnishes the material which is to shape the thoughts of our people, is essentially the man who more than any other determines the character of the people and the kind of government this people shall possess."*
> —PRESIDENT ROOSEVELT, *April 7, 1904.*

BY JOSEPH PULITZER.

THE editor of the NORTH AMERICAN REVIEW has asked me to reply to an article recently printed in its pages criticising the College of Journalism which it has been my pleasure to found and permanently to endow in Columbia University. In complying with his request I have enlarged the scope of the reply to include all other criticisms and misgivings, many honest, some shallow, some based on misunderstanding, but the most representing only prejudice and ignorance. If my comment upon these criticisms shall seem to be diffuse and perhaps repetitious, my apology is that—alas!—I am compelled to write by voice, not by pen, and to revise the proofs by ear, not by eye—a somewhat difficult task.

Some of my critics have called my scheme "visionary." If it

Foreword

Today, Joseph Pulitzer (1847–1911), an immigrant from what is today Hungary, is best known for creating the prestigious Pulitzer Prizes, awarded annually for achievements in journalism, literature and music. During his lifetime, however, his reputation more closely resembled that of today's Rubert Murdock (1931–), the Australia-born director and chairman of News Corporation, one of the largest and most oft-criticized media organizations in the world. Both men displayed the same talent for taking over failing newspapers and boosting circulation with crowd-pleasing stories that led to charges of sensationalism. Under Pulitzer, the circulation of the *World* grew forty-fold, from 15,000 to 600,000, making it for a time the largest newspaper in the United States. In cable television, Murdock did much the same with the Fox News Channel. Founded in 1996, within decade it was drawing a larger share of long-term viewers than the Cable News Network, founded in 1980.

While many stories in Pulitzer's *World* were sensationalistic, manufactured solely to increase circulation, others did what many thought newspapers ought to do. Thanks to Pulitzer, Nelly Bly (1864–1922) was able to go undercover and expose the stomach-churning horrors of the Women's Lunatic Asylum. *The New York Times* might claim the press should limit itself to "All the News that's Fit to Print," implying that some stories were unfit for the respectable. But the *World* felt the press should also engage in what Theodore Roosevelt called muckraking, which he praised by noting, "I hail as a benefactor every writer or speaker, every man who, on the platform, or in book, magazine, or newspaper, with merciless severity makes such attack, provided always that he in his turn remembers that the attack is of use only if it is absolutely truthful." (Alas, Roosevelt tried unsuccessfully to sue Pulitzer for criminal libel when the *World* exposed questionable aspects of the building of the Panama Canal.)

Pulitzer's reputation as a muckraker created problems when he offered to donate part of his fortune to found a school of journalism at Columbia University. He made his first offer in 1892, when Seth Low was the university's president, but was turned down. In 1902 a new president, Nicholas Murray Butler, was more open, as we see in the newspaper articles on pages 8–10 of this book. But enough distrust remained that Pulitzer's plan would not bear fruit until 1912, the year after his death. The delay meant the nation's first school of journalism began at the University of Missouri rather than Columbia University.

In this book we bring back into print remarks made in 1904 by Horace White, one of Pulitzer's more strident critics, followed by Pulitzer's careful response. Pulitzer's remarks played a major role in promoting the idea that, like medicine and law, journalism would benefit from a university-level professional education. In a era when the Internet is again raising questions about who is a journalist, Pulitzer is well worth reading, even by those who believe that a natural aptitude is as important as a formal education.

The World

"...lation Books Open to All."

"Circulation Books Open to All.

...ENTS ***

NEW YORK, SUNDAY, AUGUST 16 1903.

Copyright, 1903, by the Press Publishing Company, N. Y. World.

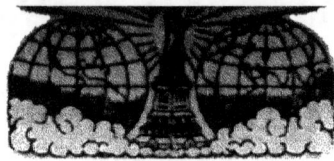

SCHOOL OF JOURNALISM FOR COLUMBIA UNIVERSITY.

Endowment of Two Million Dollars Provided by Mr. Joseph Pulitzer—Scope and Plan Announced by President Nicholas Murray Butler, of the University— Eminent Men Accept Positions on Advisory Board—New Building to Be Erected at Once on Morningside Heights.

Columbia University, of this city, is to have a School of Journalism.

Mr. Joseph Pulitzer has provided the sum of $2,000,000 for that purpose, and will erect a new building on Morningside Heights.

The University will establish and conduct a School of Journalism, which will hold toward the University a relation similar to that of the other professional schools, as the Law School, the School of Medicine and the School of Mines, and like them, will be national in scope.

An important feature of the organization of this School will be an Advisory Board, to be nominated by the donor, composed of distinguished men possessing all the knowledge and experience gained by years of successful labor. This board will aid in devising a plan and course of instruction that will meet every requirement on the scholastic as well as upon the more strictly practical side.

THE ADVISORY BOARD.

Seven members of this Advisory Board have already been designated by the donor, and, with others to be selected hereafter, will be nominated to the trustees of Columbia University at their meeting in October. These gentlemen, distinguished severally in journalism, in letters and in diplomacy, have signified their readiness heartily to co-operate in making the Columbia School of Journalism fulfil the high purpose of its founder and prove a beneficent addition to the diversified educational forces of this great university:

NICHOLAS MURRAY BUTLER, President of Columbia University, ex-officio;

Hon. WHITELAW REID;

Hon. JOHN HAY, Secretary of State;

Hon. ST. CLAIR M'KELWAY;

Hon. ANDREW D. WHITE;

*CHARLES W. ELIOT, President of Harvard University;

VICTOR F. LAWSON, of Chicago;

Gen. CHARLES H. TAYLOR, of Boston.

*President Eliot's duties in connection with his own university will prevent him from serving on the permanent Advisory Board, but he has cordially approved the plan, has given to the founder much wise counsel and will give to individual members of the Advisory Board the invaluable benefits of his great experience and knowledge.

All the others named have signified their willingness to serve on the Advisory Board.

TO FIX THE STANDARD.

By the foundation of this school it is proposed not merely to enlarge and improve the opportunities that are open to young men for a start in life, but to raise and fix the character and standard of the press itself as a moral teacher and a promoter of that publicity which makes for better government and for the advancement of civilization.

Students purposing to enter upon the career of journalism will find accessible here courses of study that will for this profession be equivalent to what other professional schools supply for other professions; while young men already engaged upon the newspapers and desiring to advance themselves more rapidly by the cultivation of their aptitudes may find in these courses a valuable assistance. It is believed that this will be an advantage to them immediately, and ultimately to the press of the whole country.

of a general survey under the heading of administration, but of detailed exposition and training in separate courses.)

NEWSPAPER MANUFACTURE—Printing presses; inks; paper; electrotyping and stereotyping processes; type composition; typesetting and typecasting machines; processes for reproducing illustrations; folding, binding and mailing devices.

THE LAW OF JOURNALISM—Copyright; libel, including civil, criminal and seditious libel; rights and duties of the press in reporting judicial proceedings; liabilities of publisher, editor, reporter and contributor.

ETHICS OF JOURNALISM—Proper sense of responsibility to the public on the part of newspaper writers; to what extent should the opinions of the editor or owner of a newspaper affect its presentation of news? Relations of publisher, editor and reporters as regards freedom of opinion.

HISTORY OF JOURNALISM—Freedom of the Press, &c.

THE LITERARY FORM OF NEWSPAPERS—Approved usages in punctuation, spelling, abbreviations, typography, &c.

RE-ENFORCEMENT OF EXISTING DEPARTMENTS OF INSTRUCTION for the benefit of students of journalism: In English—reporting of news, news-letters, reviews, paragraph writing, editorial writing; In History—emphasis on contemporary history, government and geography; In Political Science—emphasis on contemporary economic problems and financial administration.

NEW BUILDING TO BE ERECTED.

It is probable that the scheme of instruction will include several of the academic courses now taught in the University, but will also give special prominence to the other side of the study—to the endeavor to impart by thorough teaching and training what has been hitherto acquired in the hard school of actual practice. The newspaper men who will define the precise detail of this part will themselves recognize and attach a proper value to each division of this study.

A building for the School of Journalism will be erected, at the cost of half a million dollars, upon the ground owned by the University at Morningside Heights. This edifice will probably be completed by the autumn of 1904, and it is hoped that the School may be opened soon after. The course of study will be two years. Candidates will be admitted upon an examination as to good character and intelligence, but previous collegiate courses will not be required. Further details as to conditions of entrance, &c., will be made known at the proper time by the University authorities.

Columbia University's Official Statement.

The following statement is authorized by the Secretary of Columbia University:

"President Butler, of Columbia University, announced yesterday that the trustees had received a gift of one million dollars from Mr. Joseph Pulitzer, of New York, for the establishment and endowment of a School of Journalism in Columbia University. This generous gift puts into effect a purpose which Mr. Pulitzer has long had in contemplation, namely, the provision of an opportunity to secure in a great university both theoretical and practical training for journalism considered as a profession. The School of Journalism of Columbia University will take rank with the existing professional schools of law, medicine, engineering, architecture and teaching. Subject to the general jurisdiction of the University Council, its course of study will be formulated and its administration carried on by a faculty of journalism, the members of which will be appointed by the trustees in the near future.

of a general survey under the heading of administration, but of detailed exposition and training in separate courses.)

NEWSPAPER MANUFACTURE—Printing presses; inks; paper; electrotyping and stereotyping processes; type composition; typesetting and typecasting machines; processes for reproducing illustrations; folding, binding and mailing devices.

THE LAW OF JOURNALISM—Copyright; libel, including civil, criminal and seditious libel; rights and duties of the press in reporting judicial proceedings; liabilities of publisher, editor, reporter and contributor.

ETHICS OF JOURNALISM—Proper sense of responsibility to the public on the part of newspaper writers; to what extent should the opinions of the editor or owner of a newspaper affect its presentation of news? Relations of publisher, editor and reporters as regards freedom of opinion.

HISTORY OF JOURNALISM—Freedom of the Press, &c.

THE LITERARY FORM OF NEWSPAPERS—Approved usages in punctuation, spelling, abbreviations, typography, &c.

RE-ENFORCEMENT OF EXISTING DEPARTMENTS OF INSTRUCTION for the benefit of students of journalism: In English—reporting of news, news-letters, reviews, paragraph writing, editorial writing; In History—emphasis on contemporary history, government and geography; In Political Science—emphasis on contemporary economic problems and financial administration.

NEW BUILDING TO BE ERECTED.

It is probable that the scheme of instruction will include several of the academic courses now taught in the University, but will also give special prominence to the other side of the study—to the endeavor to impart by thorough teaching and training what has been hitherto acquired in the hard school of actual practice. The newspaper men who will define the precise detail of this part will themselves recognize and attach a proper value to each division of this study.

A building for the School of Journalism will be erected, at the cost of half a million dollars, upon the ground owned by the University at Morningside Heights. This edifice will probably be completed by the autumn of 1904, and it is hoped that the School may be opened soon after. The course of study will be two years. Candidates will be admitted upon an examination as to good character and intelligence, but previous collegiate courses will not be required. Further details as to conditions of entrance, &c., will be made known at the proper time by the University authorities.

Columbia University's Official Statement.

The following statement is authorized by the Secretary of Columbia University:

"President Butler, of Columbia University, announced yesterday that the trustees had received a gift of one million dollars from Mr. Joseph Pulitzer, of New York, for the establishment and endowment of a School of Journalism in Columbia University. This generous gift puts into effect a purpose which Mr. Pulitzer has long had in contemplation, namely, the provision of an opportunity to secure in a great university both theoretical and practical training for journalism considered as a profession. The School of Journalism of Columbia University will take rank with the existing professional schools of law, medicine, engineering, architecture and teaching. Subject to the general jurisdiction of the University Council, its course of study will be formulated and its administration carried on by a faculty of journalism, the members of which will be appointed by the trustees in the near future.

ARCHITECTS AT WORK ON PLANS.

"The erection of a suitable building to accommodate the new school will be begun at once, and, after conference with President Butler, Messrs. McKim, Mead & White have already undertaken the preparation of preliminary plans and sketches. A provisional site for the building has been chosen in the University quadrangle on Amsterdam avenue, immediately south of Fayerweather Hall and north of the projected building for the School of Law. It is hoped that the building may be pushed to completion so that it may be occupied in the autumn of 1904. The estimated cost of the building, fully furnished and equipped, is about $500,000.

"Both Mr. Pulitzer and Columbia University recognize that with the establishment of a School of Journalism of university grade a new academic field is entered upon, and in order that the best ability and experience of the profession of journalism may guide the new undertaking, an Advisory Board has been provided for, the first members of which are to be appointed by the University upon the nomination of Mr. Pulitzer. The President of the University is to be ex-officio a member of this Advisory Board. Mr. Pulitzer will nominate the members of this Advisory Board in time for action by the trustees of the University at their next stated meeting, on the first Monday in October.

BOARD TO MEET SOON.

"A meeting of the Advisory Board will be called as soon as possible after its members are appointed, and the fundamental principles which should govern the School of Journalism will be discussed and agreed upon. After the suggestions of the Advisory Board have been communicated to the University Council and to the trustees the work of organizing the school will proceed with all possible speed, in order that instruction may be given just as soon as the building is ready for use.

"A committee consisting of President Butler and Profs. Burgess, Peck, Brander Matthews, G. R. Carpenter and Giddings has already been appointed to frame a report for early presentation to the University Council regarding the organization and academic relations of the School of Journalism.

"The length of the proposed course in journalism and its content will be decided upon after the Advisory Board has expressed an opinion on both matters. Thorough training in written English, in logic, in the elements of economics and of political science, in the history of the United States and the contemporary history of Europe, will certainly be included. The more technical courses will comprise instruction in newspaper administration, newspaper manufacture, the law and the ethics of journalism, the history of the press and related subjects.

"Specific announcements concerning the terms of admission to the School of Journalism, the length of the course and the date at which students will be received may be expected within a few weeks.

AN ADDITIONAL MILLION DOLLARS.

"If, at the end of three years, the School of Journalism is in successful operation, Mr. Pulitzer will give to Columbia University an additional million dollars the income of one-half of which will be devoted to the maintenance of the School of Journalism. The income of the remaining half million will be expended for purposes to be hereafter agreed upon between Mr. Pulitzer and the University.

PULITZER FOUNDS JOURNALISM SCHOOL

Provides $2,000,000 for Its Institution at Columbia.

President Butler Announces the Plan and Progress So Far Made—President Eliot of Harvard Suggests Courses.

Joseph Pulitzer has provided the sum of $2,000,000 to establish a School of Journalism at Columbia University, this city. A new building for the school will be erected on Morningside Heights, at a cost of $500,000, for the school, which will hold toward the university a relation similar to that of the other professional schools, as the Law School, the School of Medicine, and the School of Mines, and, like them, will be National in scope.

An important feature of the organization of this school will be an Advisory Board, to be nominated by the donor. This board will aid in devising a plan and course of instruction that will meet every requirement on the scholastic as well as upon the more strictly practical side.

Seven members of this Advisory Board have already been designated by the donor, and, with others to be selected hereafter, will be nominated to the Trustees of Columbia University at their meeting in October. They are:

President Butler of Columbia (ex-officio,)
Whitelaw Reid,
Secretary of State Hay,
St. Clair McKelway,
Andrew D. White,
Victor F. Lawson of Chicago,
Gen. Chas. H. Taylor, Sr., of Boston,
President Eliot of Harvard.

President Eliot's duties in conection with his own university will prevent him from serving on the permanent Advisory Board, but he has cordially approved the plan, has given counsel to the founder, and will give to individual members of the Advisory Board the benefits of his experience and knowledge.

All the others named have signified their willingness to serve on the Advisory Board.

THE SCHOOL OF JOURNALISM.

BY HORACE WHITE.

IN a reply to questions addressed to me by the editor of the *World* some months ago, I said that I could see no need of a School of Journalism. I am, nevertheless, glad that Columbia University has been supplied with the means to establish one. This is not intended as a paradox. Columbia already has the plant and the teaching force for the training of journalists in so far as they can be trained otherwise than by practice; but both the plant and the teaching force are susceptible of improvement. There is no danger that they will be overloaded by the addition of one or two million dollars to the existing resources. If the authorities of Columbia are fit for their places, general culture will receive an impulse from Mr. Pulitzer's donation, and journalism will share therein.

It is quite probable, too, that the existence of this fund, and the stir that it makes in the country, will draw to Columbia more than her usual share of young men who seek to become journalists. Although Harvard or Yale, without a School of Journalism, might conceivably be better equipped to train men for editorial work than Columbia with one, yet the average boy would expect to get from the latter more of the kind of instruction that he wants than from either of the former. Then Columbia, feeling an impulse in this direction, would, no doubt, be spurred to fresh exertions in her departments of political and social science, and whatever else she might regard as most helpful to the editorial mind; and that would be a gain to general culture, including journalism.

I maintain, however, that the university has nothing to teach journalists in the special sense that it has to teach lawyers, physicians, architects and engineers. It can teach the *technique* of those professions. It cannot teach the *technique* of journalism, except by publishing a newspaper in competition with other newspapers in the same town. If it should attempt to do so, Mr. Pulitzer's money would probably be spent in less time than he took to earn it.

The art of English composition is taught in all universities, colleges, and high schools with more or less success. The desideratum here is not a school of journalism, but a good teacher. After the intending journalist has obtained as much proficiency in writing good English as he can acquire without practice under the goad of the printer's devil, his technical requirements are—what? First of all, a "nose for news." In this phrase are included the recognition, the valuation, the collection and arrangement of news. Every experienced journalist will agree that a nose for news cannot be cultivated at college. Some other kinds of noses may be, but the one which perceives immediately what kind of news the public is most eager to read, and knows offhand how to get it and present it in an attractive way—that is something which can be trained only in a newspaper office. There are differences of scent between trained newspaper men as marked as between different breeds of dogs, and the demand for journalists who are both highly gifted and highly trained in this particular, is great and increasing; but such men have never been made at college, and never will be.

What are the other technicalities of journalism? I can think of none except phonography, typewriting, and proof-reading. I have never met an editor-in-chief who was a shorthand writer. My colleague, Edwin L. Godkin, used a typewriter in the composition of editorials in his later years, but he learned the art at his own home in his leisure hours. Anybody can learn the technical part of proof-reading in two hours, although practice is needed to acquire rapidity and accuracy. Columbia would no more think of embracing these things in her curriculum than she would of establishing a chair of head-lines, a chair of interviews, or a chair of "scoops."

In their academic departments, all the colleges and universities of the country are schools of journalism, some having larger and better equipment for this task than others, just as some have larger libraries and laboratories than others. They are all supplying, in greater or less measure, the training that young men need to improve their keenness and breadth of vision, and to enable them to judge of the value of evidence (which J. S. Mill considered the chief object of education), and to express their thoughts in good English. It is not a new kind of training that Columbia will introduce in her School of Journalism, but a betterment of the kind she already gives. She could do nothing different even if Mr. Pulitzer's gift were ten times as great as it is. The fundamentals of journalism are those which we have in mind when we say that Mr. So-and-So is a gentleman and a scholar; and it is only fundamentals which the university can supply.

Of course, some ways of using the money will be better than others, and here, perhaps, a leaf out of my own experience may be useful. I entered journalism in 1854. I had received the college education in vogue at that time. It included Latin and Greek, in which I was fairly well grounded, and which I have always found useful. It did not include English. At that time English was supposed to be born, not made. This was the opinion of educators in Columbia as well as in Beloit. No college at that time gave courses in English, so far as I can discover. This was a serious defect, but it was supplemented in my case by incessant drilling in the Old and New Testaments, administered as religious, not as literary, exercises, and even more at home and in Sunday-school than in the college. It was well for me that I had this training, for I consider the English Bible the best instrument for instruction in the English tongue that exists to-day, and the best guide to the acquirement of good style of composition; yet it did not make up for the lack of Shakespeare, Milton, Burke, Goldsmith and the other English classics. It did not supply the place of a good teacher of English rhetoric and literature. Columbia is well equipped in this department, and all I need say further under this head is that it should constitute the groundwork of a journalist's training.

The next serious defect in my early education was a want of acquaintance with the science of law. I gained some notions of Roman law from Cicero's orations and moral works, but only incidentally. The only law book that entered into my curriculum was Story on the Constitution. This was good as far as it went, but it was not the bed-rock that I needed. I found myself much hampered by ignorance of the English common law, which I sought to repair by reading Kent's Commentaries, in the intervals of daily journalistic work. I thus came to know where to look for further instruction in special branches of law, as occasion required. I should recommend as an important part of a journalist's training, not only the doses of Roman law, constitutional law and international law which all universities now supply, but also a good draught of English common law.

I was well grounded in political economy (as the science then existed) by President Chapin of Beloit, himself a keen thinker and clear writer on that subject. What I acquired in college, however, was a due appreciation of economics as part of an editor's furnishings, rather than multifarious cramming. The only books I saw in college were those of Wayland and J. B. Say, the former as a text-book, the latter for private reading; but very little has appeared in books or magazines since that time that I have not mastered, or tested by sample. This I have found necessary in order to give advice to my readers on the numberless problems, of an economic sort, that are constantly arising in public affairs. Columbia is strong on the economic side and will doubtless so continue.

Neither political science nor history was taught in my college years. Greek and Roman history I had in abundance as part of my classical training; but modern history we were supposed to acquire, as we acquired English literature, by induced currents rather than direct contact. Neither sociology nor psychology existed then, although phrenology and mesmerism were much in evidence. Since my graduation, a whole troop of sciences have pushed forward which may justly claim a place in the young journalist's curriculum; and here is room for sound judgment, and discrimination on the part of Columbia's committee on organization. Their aim should be to make a gentleman and a scholar in every case, and leave him to learn journalism afterwards by practice.

How to produce the scholar for journalism has been sufficiently indicated. How to produce the gentleman is something different and not always attainable. The formation of character begins earlier than college life, but continues through it and long after. It does not end while life lasts. American colleges and universities without exception do aim to give their students correct moral, as well as intellectual, training. They do strive to make them good citizens. Now, the high-minded man and good citizen will be such in all times and places, whatever be his walk in life. The same rules will govern him in the editorial chair, or at the reporter's desk, that would govern him in the pulpit or in the counting-room. Lectureships have been established in some institutions lately on the duties of the citizen. These are to be commended, but they apply to all trades and professions as fully as to journalism.

The question arises at this point, why are there so many black sheep in journalism? Why so many "fakes"? Why is the epidemic of "yellow journalism" so prevalent? This phrase is applied to newspapers which delight in sensations, crime, scandal, smut, funny pictures, caricatures and malicious or frivolous gossip about persons and things of no public concern. When I entered journalism, the press of the country, with only one exception that I can now recall, was clean, dignified and sober-minded. It had various aims in life, aims political, literary, scientific, social, religious, reformatory and mixed, which were deemed by the conductors of the papers advantageous to the common weal. To make money by pandering to the vices and follies of the community, and thus adding to the mass of vice and folly, was generally unthinkable.

The yellow journalist, when somebody remonstrates against his practices, says that the fault lies with the public taste; that he merely gives the people what they want. This means that he has made experiments on the public appetite, and has found that he can get more dollars by spreading folly and foulness through the community than by publishing decent news in a decent way. In like manner, others have found that they can make more money by keeping pool rooms and disorderly houses than by following the plough or sawing wood. Yet when we have said this—when we have heaped anathemas on the head of the yellow journalist—we have not advanced an inch toward betterment. We stand confronted with the fact that it pays to publish this kind of newspaper, and that, as long as it pays, this kind of newspaper will be published. I once believed that people would soon tire of such vulgarity and nonsense, and that yellow journalism would cease for want of a market, but I confess that I do not yet see any natural law in operation to check its desolating career. On the other hand, I do see that the public takes less interest in thoughtful discussions of serious questions in the press than it did when I first entered the profession. The reason is that it gets less of it. Mental activity grows by what it feeds on. If the thinking faculty is not kept in practice, it falls into noxious desuetude.

The vice which consists in making newspapers marketable rather than good is not wholly confined to the yellow journals. It is found in a tendency to eschew " heaviness " of all kinds; to avoid articles which require thought to produce and to appreciate; and especially to steer clear of all blizzards and fog-banks of public opinion which might temporarily chill the circulation. This spirit is found in very respectable newspapers. Their aim is to be light, breezy and picturesque, perhaps grotesque, and to give offence to nobody. " Modern journalism," says Mr. E. L. Shuman in an acute and valuable work,* " has higher rewards for those who can amuse than for those whose main object is to instruct." The bad rich press and the timid rich press are like King Stork and King Log to the frog community. In saying this I do not lose sight of some fine examples of the independent press, which still flourish; but I affirm that the press of fifty years ago was, as a whole, stronger intellectually, more influential and more respected than the press is now, although, in the mere matter of news-gathering, it was as inferior to the press of to-day as a blacksmith's forge is to the Carnegie steel works.

I chanced the other day to pick up the " Recollections " of the actor Stoddart, containing an Introduction by William Winter, who says therein that " in acting, as well as in literature, fine and substantial things—things having in them the grandeur of noble truth and the fire of genial passion—were more frequent forty or fifty years ago than they are now. The actor of the old school," he continues, " was an actor thoroughly grounded in his profession, trained by experience, equipped at all points, able to do many things well and some things brilliantly, and, whatever may have been his defects, solid and stable in character, moderate in self-confidence and usually modest in the conduct of life." I agree with Mr. Winter in this. The editor and the actor of half a century ago were keyed to the same pitch, and I cannot help asking myself whether the decadence of the press has not had something to do with the decadence of the stage. The people take the kind of newspaper that is given to them, and nine-tenths of

* " Practical Journalism," by E. L. Shuman, New York, 1903.

them are unconsciously cast in its mould. If it is mentally ener-
vating and silly, they will be so; if it is yellow, they will reflect the
same hue.

The sum and substance of my theme is, that yellow journalism
exists because it pays and that it pays because it exists. How to
disable this machine of perpetual motion is the greatest problem
that confronts our social philosophers. It exceeds in importance
the Philippine question, or the race question, or the municipal
government question. It includes all these and much more. I
have seen the American people recover their balance in many fear-
ful crises, when they seemed on the point of toppling over; but I
can imagine one in which the Republic might receive great detri-
ment without the people knowing what hurt them, or even knowing that they were hurt. If such a calamity comes it will come
through bad journalism, not a subsidized press but a brain-soften-
ing press, such as we have now in large and growing measure.

"It is well to remember," says Mr. Shuman, "that the editorial department is dwindling, while the great currents of life
that sweep nightly through the reportorial departments are increasing yearly." It is a fact that good political writers are
scarcer now than they were fifty years ago. It is harder to obtain
them now than then, harder now than at any other time in my experience. The colleges are sending out larger numbers of graduates and more highly-trained ones, yet the number seeking posi-
tions as editorial writers, and qualified, or showing aptitude,
therefor is smaller than it has ever been in my time. There must
be a reason for this. Among the drolleries of the day I saw not
long ago a question and answer like the following: "Why are good
cooks and waitresses so scarce?" "Because they are engaged in
writing stories for the magazines. It pays better."

In all branches of personal service, demand and supply usually
keep in close touch with each other, and this is especially true
of intellectual service. If the supply of good editorial writers
has fallen off, it must be because the demand has fallen off, and
this, I believe, is the truth. I mean the kind of demand that calls
into being an effective and regular supply. No self-respecting
youth will prepare himself for future connection with a yellow
journal; and, in general, the number who will prepare for newspaper work will be governed by the aspect in which journalism
daily presents itself to their eyes. What are the most prominent

features of journalism to-day? They are pictures, head-lines, color scheme, job type, sports, gossip. Is it any wonder that the bright young men, those who feel "growing pains" for high achievement and growing hope for distinction therein, are re-pelled from a profession which presents itself to them in such harlequin garb? But that is not all. In order that there may be a steady supply of good editorial writers, there must be both a congenial field for them to work in and a sufficient fund to pay them. But the money formerly destined for the editorial writer now goes to the cartoonist, the artist reporter, and the color schemer. Does any one ask why good editorial writers are so scarce nowadays? May they not be employed as waiters at hotels and restaurants, finding the occupation there more congenial and the pay more regular?

To make good journalists is not difficult. The raw material abounds and the tools are not deficient. But to do noble work of preparation they must see a field of labor worthy of noble minds. Show them an arena where the highest merit will win the highest prize, as in law, medicine and engineering, and the arena will soon be vocal with the *gaudium certaminis.*

HORACE WHITE.

The School of Journalism

in

Columbia University

The Power of Public Opinion

By

JOSEPH PULITZER

Published by
Columbia University
in the City of New York
Morningside Heights
New York, N. Y.

The School of Journalism in Columbia University[1]

A Review of Criticisms and Objections — Reflections Upon the Power, the Progress and the Prejudices of the Press—Why Specialized Concentration and Education at College Would Improve the Character and Work of Journalists and So Promote the Welfare of the Republic.

" The man who writes, the man who month in and month out, week in and week out, day in and day out, furnishes the material which is to shape the thoughts of our people, is essentially the man who more than any other determines the character of the people and the kind of government this people shall possess."—PRESIDENT ROOSEVELT, April 7, 1904.

THE editor of *The North American Review* has asked me to reply to an article recently printed in its pages criticising the College of Journalism which I have endowed as part of Columbia University. In complying with his request I have enlarged the scope of the reply to include all other criticisms and misgivings, many honest, some shallow, some based on misunderstanding, but the most representing only prejudice and ignorance. If my comment upon these criticisms shall seem to be diffuse and perhaps repetitious, my apology is that—alas!—I am compelled to write by voice, not pen, and to revise the proofs by ear, not eye— a somewhat difficult task.

[1] Reprinted by special permission from *The North American Review* for May, 1904. Copyright, 1904, by the North American Review Publishing Co.

Some of my critics have called my scheme "visionary." If it be so I can at least plead that it is a vision I have cherished long, thought upon deeply and followed persistently. Twelve years ago I submitted the idea to President Low of Columbia, but it was not accepted by the Trustees. I have ever since continued to perfect and organize the scheme in my mind, and now it is adopted. In examining the criticisms and misgivings I have been anxious only to find the truth. I admit that the difficulties are many, but after weighing them all impartially I am more firmly convinced than ever of the ultimate success of the idea. Before the century closes schools of journalism will be generally accepted as a feature of specialized higher education, like schools of law or of medicine.

And now for our critics and objectors :

Must a Journalist Be "Born"? They object, the critics and cavillers, that a "newspaper man" must depend solely upon natural aptitude, or, in the common phrase, that he must be "born, not made."

Perhaps the critics can name some great editor, born full-winged like Mercury, the messenger of the gods? I know of none. The only position that occurs to me which a man in our Republic can successfully fill by the simple fact of birth is that of an idiot. Is there any other position for which a man does not demand and receive training—training at home, training in schools and colleges, training by master craftsmen, or training through bitter experience—through the burns that make the child dread the fire, through blunders costly to the aspirant?

This last is the process by which the profession of journalism at present obtains its recruits. It works by natural selection and the survival of the fittest, and its failures are strewn along the wayside.

The "born editor" who has succeeded greatly without special

preparation is simply a man with unusual ability and aptitude for his chosen profession, with great power of concentration and sustained effort. He is one who loves his work and puts his whole heart and mind into it. He is in the strictest sense an educated man, but he has merely substituted *self*-education for education by others, making up for any deficiencies in his training by the unreserved sacrifice of strength, energy and pleasure. Even in his case might it not be an advantage to have a system of instruction that would give him the same results at a saving of much time and labor ?

Education begins in the cradle, at home, with a mother's teaching, and is continued by other influences through life. A college is one of those influences—useful, but with no magical power. A fool trailing an alphabet of degrees after his name is still a fool ; and a genius, if necessary, will make his own college, although with a painful waste of effort which might be better reserved for productive work. I seem to remember that Lincoln, whose academy was a borrowed book read by the light of a pine-knot on the hearth, studied Euclid in Congress when nearly forty. But would it not have been better if that work had been done at fourteen ?

All intelligence requires development. The highest profits by it; the lowest is helpless without it. Shakespeare's best play, *Hamlet,* was not his first, but his nineteenth, written after growth and maturity—after the hard work, the experience, the exercise of faculties and the accumulation of knowledge gained by writing eighteen plays. As Shakespeare was a " born " genius, why did he not write *Hamlet* first ?

John Stuart Mill had natural talents, but they were strained to the last possible limit of accomplishment by a course of early training that was not only thorough but inhuman. His father was his college—a great college, better than any in England. Like Mill, Herbert Spencer, Buckle, Huxley, Tyndall and Lewes were without college education, but their mental discipline was most severe. Cobden was undoubtedly a genius born, but if we compare his original style—turgid, clumsy—with the masterly clearness and force of his trained maturity, can we doubt that his brain was developed by the hardest work, just as Sandow's muscles were developed?

Of course in every field natural aptitude is the key to success. When the experiment was tried of turning Whistler into a disciplined soldier even West Point had to lay down its arms. Your sawmill may have all the modern improvements, but it will not make a pine board out of a basswood log. No college can create a good lawyer without a legal mind to work on, nor make a successful doctor of a young man whom nature designed to sell tape. Talleyrand took holy orders, but they did not turn him into a holy man.

The great general, even more than the great editor, is supposed to be born, not made. The picturesque historian tells us that he "fell like a thunderbolt upon the enemy," and we imagine a miracle-working magician. But the truth is that the brilliant general is simply a man who has learned how to apply skilfully the natural laws of force, and who has the nerve to act on his knowledge. Hannibal, the greatest of all in my opinion, is called a typical example of native military genius. But can we forget that he was the son and pupil of Hamilcar, the ablest soldier of his generation, born in the camp, never outside the military atmosphere, sworn in earliest boyhood to war and hatred of Rome and endowed by his father with all the military knowledge that the experience of antiquity could give? He was educated. In his father he had a military college to himself. Can we think of Napoleon without

4

remembering that he had the best military education of his time at the college of Brienne, and that he was always an eager student of the great campaigns of history ? Frederick the Great lost his head in his first battle. It took him years to learn his trade and finally to surpass his instructors. There is not a cadet at any military school who is not expected as a necessary part of his professional preparation to study every important battle on record— to learn how it was fought, what mistakes were committed on each side and how it was won.

Every issue of a newspaper represents a battle—a battle for excellence. When the editor reads it and compares it with its rivals he knows that he has scored a victory or suffered a defeat. Might not the study of the most notable of these battles of the press be as useful to the student of journalism as is the study of military battles to the student of war ?

They object that news instinct must be born.

Certainly. But however great a gift, if news instinct as born were turned loose in any newspaper office in New York without the control of sound judgment bred by considerable experience and training, the results would be much more pleasing to the lawyers than to the editor. One of the chief difficulties in journalism now is to keep the news instinct from running rampant over the restraints of accuracy and conscience. And if "a nose for news" is born in the cradle, does not the instinct, like other great qualities, need development by teaching, by training, by practical object-lessons illustrating the good and the bad, the Right and the Wrong, the popular and the unpopular, the things that succeed and the things that fail, and, above all, the things that deserve to succeed and the things that do not—not the things only that make circulation for to-day, but the things that make character and influence and public confidence ?

Can Conscience Be Developed?

" Of the ends to be kept in view by the legislator, all are unimportant compared to the end of ' character-making.' This alone is national education."—HERBERT SPENCER.

They object that moral character, like news instinct, cannot be made, but must be born. This is a very serious objection, for to me an editor without moral character has nothing. But is it entirely true? Have not the critics themselves reached their present moral altitude by degrees? Training cannot create temperament, I admit, nor perhaps radically change it; but is not conscience different from temperament? Is it not largely a question of education? May it not be considered more an acquired than an inherited or inherent quality? Is there not some reason to believe that conscience is largely a question of climate and geography? As Macaulay said: " Child murder in London leads to the scaffold; on the Ganges it is an honored religious sacrifice." A Hindu widow who burned herself to death on her husband's funeral pyre was performing the highest duty imposed by her moral sense. The English regarded her sacrifice as not only a crime, but the act of an incredible fool, and suppressed it in callous disregard of the protests of her shocked conscience.

Many an English or American married woman not only regards widowhood without any of those feelings of horror that led her Hindu sister to cut it short on the funeral pile—she often anticipates it by the help of the divorce courts, and enjoys the pleasing sensation of being the legal widow of more than one man at the same time. The missionary feels no profounder complacency in converting the cannibal than the cannibal feels in eating the missionary. A Kentucky mountaineer will commit murder, but he will not steal; a ward politician will often steal, but he will not, as a rule, commit murder. In Turkey a man may with a clear conscience have several wives; in Tibet a woman may have several husbands; in America nobody may have more than one

27

husband or wife in good legal standing at a time. If George Washington had been kidnapped in infancy and reared by thieves in a slum, with a thief for his only instructor instead of the devout mother who trained him in morals and religion, is it likely that he would have grown up the Washington whom we love and revere as the father of his country?

They object that moral courage cannot be taught. Very true. I admit that it is the hardest thing in the world to teach. But may we not be encouraged by the reflection that physical courage is taught? It is not to be supposed that every young man who enters West Point or Annapolis, Brienne, St. Cyr or Sandhurst is a born hero. Yet the student at any of these schools is so drilled, hammered and braced in the direction of courage that by the time he graduates it is morally certain that when he takes his men under fire for the first time he will not flinch. Pride and the spirit of emulation can make masses of men do what even a hero would not venture to do alone. Is it likely that Napoleon himself would have charged in solitary grandeur across the bridge at Lodi if there had been no one to see him do it? Or would Pickett's brigade at Gettysburg have gone forward to destruction if every man in it had not been lifted out of himself by the feeling that he and his comrades were all doing a heroic thing together—a thing in which he simply could not do less than the rest?

If such things can be done for physical courage, why not for moral courage? If the mind can be taught to expose the body fearlessly to wounds and death, cannot the soul be taught to cling to its convictions against temptation, prejudice, obloquy and persecution? Moral courage is developed by experience and by teaching. Every successful exercise of it makes the next easier. The editor is often confronted by an apparent dilemma—either to yield to a popular passion that he feels to be wrong or to risk the consequences of unpopularity. Adherence to convictions can and should be taught by precept and example as not only high principle but sound policy. Might not a hundred concrete examples of inflexible devotion to the right serve as a moral tonic to the student ?

Must Journalism Be Learned in the Office ? They object that such making as a newspaper man needs after he has been successfully born can be done only in the actual practice of the office, or " shop."

What is the actual practice of the office ? It is not intentional, but only incidental training ; it is not apprenticeship — it is work, in which every participant is supposed to know his business. Nobody in a newspaper office has the time or the inclination to teach a raw reporter the things he ought to know before taking up even the humblest work of the journalist. That is not what editors are doing. One of the learned critics remarks that Greeley took young Raymond in hand and hammered him into a great editor. True. But was it not an expensive process, as well as an unusual one — the most distinguished newspaper-maker of his time turning himself into a college of journalism for the benefit of a single pupil ? Suppose a man of half Greeley's capacity, set free from the exhausting labors and the harassing perplexities of creating a newspaper every day — relieved from the necessity of correcting the blunders of subordinates, of watching to prevent the perpetration of more blunders, and able to concentrate his whole heart and soul upon training his pupils — might he not be able to turn out, not one Raymond, but forty ?

Incidentally, I venture to mention that in my own experience as a newspaper reporter and editor I never had one single lesson from anybody.

The " shop" idea is the one that used to prevail in the law and in medicine. Legal studies began by copying bills of costs for the country lawyer; medical training by sweeping out a doctor's office. Now it is recognized that better results are obtained by starting with a systematic equipment in a professional school. The lawyer learns. nothing at college except the theory of the law, its principles and some precedents. When he receives his diploma he is quite unprepared to practise. Nor does the doctor learn to practise at the medical school. He learns only principles, theories, rules, the experience of others — the foundation of his profession. After leaving college he must work in the hospitals to acquire the art of practically applying his knowledge.

In journalism at present the newspaper offices are the hospitals, but the students come to them knowing nothing of principles or theories. The newspaper hospital is extremely accommodating. It furnishes the patients for its young men to practise on, puts dissecting-knives into the hands of beginners who do not know an artery from a vermiform appendix and pays them for the blunders by which they gradually teach themselves their profession. We may sympathize with the students in their industrious efforts at self-education, but may we not also sympathize with the unfortunate editor who has to work with such incompetent instruments?

" To rear up minds with aspirations and faculties above the herd, capable of leading on their country-men to greater achievement in virtue, intelligence and general well-being—these are the ends for which endowed universities are desirable ; they are those which all endowed universities profess to aim at, and great is their disgrace if, having undertaken this task and claiming credit for fulfilling it, they leave it unfulfilled."—John Stuart Mill.

Is a New College Superfluous ?

They object that even if a college education be desirable everything needed is already provided in the existing colleges and no special department is required.

This criticism appears to have some force. It is possible that it may be advanced with sincerity by intelligent newspaper men who know nothing of colleges, or by intelligent college men who know nothing of newspapers. But it is superficial. It is true that many of the subjects needed for the general education of a journalist are already covered in college. But they are too much covered. The student of journalism may find one course in a law school, another in a graduate school of political science, another, at the same hour, in an undergraduate class at college and another in a department of literature.

A young man of very remarkable gifts—enough to enable him to educate himself without the help of a college—might be able to make from the immensely bulky and intricate catalogue a selection of courses which would appear on paper to be a very fair curriculum. It would perhaps be adequate if he could keep the studies from conflicting in hours, which he could not, and if at twenty years of age he already possessed that knowledge of the requirements of his chosen profession which I feel that nearly twice twenty years' experience and hard work in my profession have not given me.

But after this wonderful young man has made out his list of studies he will be doomed to disappointment. The courses in history, in law, in political science and the rest will not be what he really needs as a specialist in journalism. They will give him only a fraction of the knowledge he requires on those subjects, and they will swamp that fraction in a flood of details of which he can make no use. To fit these courses to his purpose they must be remodelled and specialized. Modern industry looks sharply after its by-products. In silver-mining, gold is sometimes found as a by-product exceeding the value of the silver. So in general university courses we may find by-products that would meet the needs of the journalist. Why not divert, deflect, extract, concentrate, *specialize them for the journalist as a specialist?*

The spirit of specialization is everywhere. The lawyer is a real-estate lawyer, or a criminal lawyer, or a corporation lawyer, or possibly a criminal-corporation lawyer. Formerly the family physician treated every ailment; now there are specialists for the eye, the ear, the throat, the teeth; for men, for women, for children; even for imaginary diseases; for every possible variety of practice. And there is specialization in the newspaper offices themselves. The editor of a New York paper confined to the editorial page is as much surprised as the reader when in the morning he reads the news columns. The news editor does not know what editorials there will be; the musical critic could not write of sporting events; the man with the priceless sense of humor could not record and interpret the movements of the stock-market. The men in all these fields are specialists. The object of the College of Journalism will be to dig through this general scheme intended to cover every possible career or work in life, every profession, to select and concentrate only upon the things which the journalist wants, and not to waste time on things that he does not want.

They object that a college of journalism would establish class distinctions in the profession — an invidious distinction of the few who had received the benefits of a collegiate training against the many who had not enjoyed this advantage. I sincerely hope it will create a class distinction between the fit and the unfit. We need a class feeling among journalists — one based not upon money but upon morals, education and character. Class Distinctions—Why Not?

There are still a few places in which money is not everything, and they are those in which men are joined by a bond of honorable association. The cadet at West Point is taught honor and pride in his profession. He knows that none of his comrades will lie or cheat or do anything unworthy of a gentleman, and the pleasure he feels in such associations fully compensates for his ridiculously small income. He sees thousands of vulgar people, much more prosperous than himself, living in much greater luxury, yet he would not change his life and his social circle for theirs. May we not hope that a similar education will in the future create a similar corps feeling among journalists — the same pride in the profession, the same determination to do nothing "unbecoming an officer and a gentleman"? Why not?

The journalist has a position that is all his own. He alone has the privilege of moulding the opinion, touching the hearts and appealing to the reason of hundreds of thousands every day. Here is the most fascinating of all professions. The soldier may wait forty years for his opportunity. Most lawyers, most physicians, most clergymen die in obscurity, but every single day opens new doors for the journalist who holds the confidence of the community and has the capacity to address it.

But as yet the journalist works alone. If he is a college graduate he goes to his college club as a graduate, not as a journalist. He never speaks of another journalist as "my colleague," as the lawyer or the physician does of his professional brother. He hardly ever meets other journalists socially in any numbers. But if the future editors of the city were in large proportion graduates of the same college and had a recognized professional meeting-place in which they could come together informally and discuss matters of common interest, would they not eventually develop a professional pride that would enable them to work in concert for the public good and that would put any black sheep of the profession in a very uncomfortable position? Such a spirit would be the surest guaranty against the control of the press by powerful financial interests — not an imaginary danger by any means.

If such a class spirit existed no editor who had degraded him-self by becoming the hireling of any Wall Street king or ring would dare to face his colleagues. He would be too conscious of having been false to his better nature and equally false to the traditions of his college and of his profession. It would be impossible then for any Huntington or Gould of the next generation to buy up newspapers — a thing easily feasible where hundreds of millions are at stake unless there is a strong feeling of class pride and principle to prevent it. The knowledge that a reputable journalist would refuse to edit any paper that represented private interest against the public good would be enough of itself to discourage such an enterprise. Such a refusal would be as severe a blow to public confidence in the newspaper as the rejection of a brief by a high-minded lawyer is to the standing of a case in court.

No, there is nothing to fear in class distinctions founded on moral and mental superiority — on education and knowledge. We need more such classes, in the presence of the prevailing mania for mere money-making. The million of teachers form a class of this kind, with small pay, but with the consciousness of pursuing a noble profession. Such distinctions are especially necessary in a republic which has discarded everything in the way of rank and title and left personal merit the only thing that can dispute the worship of wealth.

They object that schools of journalism have been tried and have failed. This is very shallow, and while technically true is practically untrue. There are persons occupying desk-room in grimy offices who advertise to make journalists to order. There are more pretentious "correspondence schools" which tell, no doubt correctly, how to read proof and prepare copy for the press. And there have even been certain courses of lectures in

Has the Experiment Been Tried?

colleges and universities of standing, in which gentlemen of more or less extensive experience in journalism have expressed some general ideas about the requirements of the profession. This thus far has been the Lilliputian limit of effort in the direction of a university training for journalism.

So far as these could have any effect at all it would be in the direction of convincing the student that he would do better to choose some other profession. One lecturer, who is an exceedingly successful and able magazine editor, devoted his time to explaining the value of fiction and the "market" for short stories. He treated newspapers solely from the commercial point of view and never once referred to their ethical side.

Something has been said of a so-called school of journalism in London, which is compared with the proposed institution at Columbia. I do not wish to disparage the London school, but it has about ten boys,—not college students, just schoolboys,—and its whole endowment is one travelling scholarship. I may mention incidentally that there will be five travelling scholarships at Columbia. To compare a boys' school or a few desultory courses of lectures with a college amply and permanently endowed and equipped in a great university is preposterous. Instruction in journalism has never yet had a fair chance to show what it can do. The new institution will be the first experiment of its kind.

How Will Teachers Be Found? They object that competent teachers, without whom the most ingenious plans of instruction must fail, are not to be found. I confess that this is the greatest, gravest difficulty and danger. Like any college, we must have in the first place a combination of the highest character and capacity, with love of and aptitude for teaching. Even this is no small thing to ask, as the difficulty of the colleges in finding suitable professors may warn us. But we need something beyond and much rarer than this.

Teachers of journalism should also be experienced editors. But how are we to lure a truly able editor from the active work of the profession in which there is such splendid scope for his powers and such eager competition for his services while he is in the prime of life ?

The difficulty of drawing the right men from active service suggests the possibility that it may be necessary to fall back upon retired editors, who can no longer take part in the strenuous newspaper life. But my hope is that the whole profession will see in this situation an appeal to its honor and its pride. I hope that the very difficulty of the problem will prove its own solution, by enlisting the sympathetic interest and aid of the men of power and of energy who would not waste their time on work that others could do. These men could not shirk the responsibilities of leadership if they would, nor do I believe they would if they could.

The greatest painters of Paris visit the art schools and criticise the work of the pupils. The masters of the New York bar give lectures in the law schools. The most famous physicians teach in the medical colleges. Why should the greatest editors not have an equally unselfish pride in and love of their own profession ? Upon their generous sympathy and aid will depend the success of the experiment.

Nor need we confine our search to journalists. Historians like McMaster, Wilson and Rhodes ; college presidents like Eliot, Hadley and Angell; judges like Fuller, Brewer and Gray — could help the work with lectures and suggestions. It is nothing new for a justice of the Supreme Court to lecture in college. Justice Story did it at Harvard, Justice Field did it at the University of California, Justices Harlan and Brewer do it now at the Columbian University at Washington. Even ex-Presidents have not thought such work belittling. Harrison lectured at Stanford and Cleveland

36

at Princeton. And surely the greatest minds of the nation must realize how indissolubly a pure republic is linked with an upright press. National pride will, I fully trust, constrain them to do what they can for the elevation of an agency by which the destinies of the Union are so profoundly affected for good or for evil.

Unteachable Things " Our taste is improved exactly as we improve our judgment, by extending our knowledge, by a steady attention to one object, and by frequent exercise."—BURKE on " The Sublime and Beautiful."

They object there are some things that a college of journalism cannot teach. I admit it. No college can give imagination, initiative, impulses, enthusiasm, a sense of humor or irony. These things must be inborn. But would not such inborn qualities be developed and strengthened in the atmosphere of the proposed college? Is not the development of such inborn qualities seen everywhere in intellectual life? The poet, it is true, is born, not made. That is also true of a great orator and a great painter. But does not the great poet indicate and cultivate his inborn genius by instinctively devouring, even as a child, all the poetry he can procure? Keats wrote: "I long to feast upon old Homer as we have upon Shakespeare and as I have lately upon Milton." Did not such orators as Demosthenes, Cicero, Burke and Webster declaim the masterpieces of oratory and rhetoric? Did not Van Dyck and every other great painter benefit by the careful study of the work of their great predecessors in art? And with these facts in mind may we not hope that the student at Columbia, living in an atmosphere of journalism, with the highest examples and ideals of journalism constantly before him, will bring to the highest efficiency whatever dormant or inborn faculty he may possess? It seems to me that the more conclusively the critics prove certain things to be unteachable the more they prove the necessity of teaching everything possible that *is* teachable.

This is all that any education can do, and it is enough. Education is development, not creation. If its value depended upon its ability to bring mental qualities into existence from nothing every educational institution from the kindergarten to the university would have to close its doors and every educator would be out of employment.

In short, does not every mental worker, whether creative or imitative, try to steep himself in the atmosphere of his work? And is it not reasonable to suppose that our student would gain some advantage from living and working for some years in the atmosphere of journalistic training?

Finally, they object that I have proved a college course in journalism to be unnecessary by succeeding without one. Perhaps I may be permitted to judge of that. It is ingenious to use me as a club against my own plan. If I have had any success it has been because I never, so far as my individual work and pleasure are concerned, regarded journalism as a business. From my first hour's work, through a period of nearly forty years, I have regarded journalism not only as a profession, but as the noblest of all professions. I have always felt that I was in touch with the public mind and ought to do some good every day. Probably I have failed, but it has not been for lack of effort.

What Should Not Be Taught

"The journalist's opportunity is beyond estimate. To him are given the keys of every study, the entry to every family, the ear of every citizen when at ease and in his most receptive moods—powers of approach and of persuasion beyond those of the Protestant pastor or the Catholic confessor. He is by no means a prophet, but, reverently be it said, he is a voice in the wilderness preparing the way. He is by no means a priest, but his words carry wider and further than the priest's, and he preaches the gospel of humanity. He is not a king, but he nurtures and trains the king, and the land is ruled by the public opinion he evokes and shapes. If you value this good land the Lord has given us, if you would have a share in this marvellous civilization and lifting power of humanity, look well to the nurture and training of your king."—HON. WHITELAW REID.

Not to teach typesetting, not to explain the methods of business management, not to reproduce with trivial variations the course of a commercial college. This is not university work. It needs no endowment. It is the idea of work for the community, not commerce, not for one's self, but primarily for the public, that needs to be taught. The School of Journalism is to be, in my conception, not only not commercial, but anti-commercial. It is to exalt principle, knowledge, culture, at the expense of business if need be. It is to set up ideals, to keep the counting-room in its proper place, and to make the soul of the editor the soul of the paper. Incidentally I may say that I have never spent an hour in any publication office either of the St. Louis *Post-Dispatch* or *The World,* though I established both these journals and still own them.

In the proposed course of study, drawn up with admirable quickness, but tentatively, by President Eliot and widely discussed as if it had been definitely adopted, Dr. Eliot included instruction in the business administration of a newspaper. He mentioned specifically circulation, advertising, manufacture and finance.

My own ideas upon many parts of the course of study are still uncertain, but upon this one point they are very decided. I am sure that if my wishes are to be considered business instruction of any sort should not, would not and must not form any part of the work of the College of Journalism.

The course of instruction will be decided by the Advisory Board, which is not yet appointed, acting in conjunction with the authorities of the university.

I have the greatest admiration for the extraordinary genius and character of the president of Harvard, but nothing was further from my mind—nothing, in fact, is more inconsistent and incompatible with my intentions or repugnant to my feelings—than to include any of the business or commercial elements of a newspaper in what is to be taught in this department of Columbia College.

What is a college of journalism ? It is an institution to train journalists. What is a journalist ? Not any business manager or publisher, or even proprietor. A journalist is the lookout on the bridge of the ship of state. He notes the passing sail, the little things of interest that dot the horizon in fine weather. He reports the drifting castaway whom the ship can save. He peers through fog and storm to give warning of dangers ahead. He is not thinking of his wages or of the profits of his owners. He is there to watch over the safety and the welfare of the people who trust him.

Few men in the business office of a newspaper know anything about the principles of journalism. The proprietor himself is not necessarily a journalist. He may be if he is capable of understanding public questions, of weighing public interests, of carrying out public tasks ; if he is in touch with public feeling, realizes public duties, is in sympathy with the public welfare, and is capable of presenting his ideas to the people, either by his own pen or by the pens of others. But it is quite conceivable that some proprietors are very deficient in these points.

My hope is that this College of Journalism will raise the standard of the editorial profession. But to do this it must mark the distinction between real journalists and men who do a kind of newspaper work that requires neither knowledge nor conviction, but merely business training. I wish to begin a movement that will raise journalism to the rank of a learned profession, growing in the respect of the community as other professions far less important to the public interests have grown.

There is an obvious difference between a business and a profession. An editor, an editorial writer or a correspondent is not in business. Nor is even a capable reporter. These men are already in a profession, though they may not admit it or even realize it, as many of them, unhappily, do not. Ill or well, they represent authorship, and authorship is a profession.

The man in the counting-room of a newspaper is in the newspaper business. He concentrates his brain (quite legitimately) upon the commercial aspects of things, upon the margin of profit, upon the reduction of expenses, upon buying white paper and selling it printed—and that is business. But a man who has the advantage, honor and pleasure of addressing the public every day as a writer or thinker is a professional man. So, of course, is he who directs these writers and reporters, who tells them what to say and how to say it, who shows them how to think—who inspires them, though he may never write a line himself, and decides what the principles and objects of the paper shall be. For example, the greatest editor in the whole history of European journalism, John Delane, never wrote any articles of his own, although for thirty-six years he was the head, the heart, the brain of the *London Times.* But he directed every writer, he furnished the thought, the policy, the initiative ; he bore the responsibility, and he corrected both manuscript and proofs.

In this relation perhaps it may be interesting to note that Delane studied law and was admitted to the bar before he became its editor at the age of twenty-four. But it was without any intention of practising. His father, who was a lawyer for the *Times,* destined him for its service from his boyhood, and he joined its staff as a reporter soon after passing his legal examinations. Delane, with his editorial revision, elimination and substitution, was like some of the great old painters, who had much of their work, measured by mere bulk, done for them by pupils. Rubens, or Van Dyck, or Raphael furnished the idea, the design, the composition, in an original drawing ; the pupils did the bulk of the execution. Then the artist added the finishing touches that lifted the picture to the rank of a masterpiece. Only in that way could the enormous output ascribed to those masters have been produced. So it was with Delane, and so it is with every editor who knows how to make the most of his powers.

That a newspaper, however great as a public institution and a public teacher, must also be a business is not to be denied, but there is nothing exceptional in this. Elements of business, of economy, of income and outgo, are in the government of the city, the State, the nation, in art, in every school, in every college, in every university, indeed, in every church. But a bishop, even though he receives pay for his work, is not regarded as a business man ; nor is a great artist, though he charge the highest possible price for his paintings and die as rich as Meissonier or Rubens. Many distinguished lawyers, such as Mr. Tilden,—one of the greatest,—were shrewd business men, able probably to outwit the majority of publishers, yet they were rightly considered members of an intellectual profession.

George Washington had extraordinary business capacity. By intelligent economy, method, sound judgment and the closest attention to details he accumulated the greatest American fortune of his time. Yet when he was called to serve the country in the field he did it without a salary. At Mount Vernon he was a business man ; in history he is a soldier, a statesman and the father of his country.

To sum up, the banker or broker, the baker or the candlestick-maker is in business—in trade. But the artist, the statesman, the thinker, the writer—all who are in touch with the public taste and mind, whose thoughts reach beyond their own livelihood to some public interest—are in professions.

Dangers of Plutocracy and Demagogy

"Our improvement is in proportion to our purpose."—MARCUS AURELIUS.

Nothing less than the highest ideals, the most scrupulous anxiety to do right, the most accurate knowledge of the problems it has to meet and a sincere sense of its moral responsibility will save journalism from subservience to business interests, seeking selfish ends antagonistic to the public welfare. For instance, Jay Gould once owned the principal Democratic newspaper of America. He had obtained it from Col. "Tom" Scott in a trade for the Texas Pacific Railroad, and I was fortunate enough to be able to relieve him of his unprofitable burden. C. P. Huntington bought a New York newspaper and turned it into a Democratic organ, he himself, like Gould, being an ardent Republican. He hoped in this way to influence Mr. Cleveland's administration and the Democrats in Congress against making the Pacific railroads pay their debts of about $120,000,000 to the Government. Incidentally he testified under oath that his journalistic experiment cost him over a million dollars, although his newspaper was so obscure that its utterances were hardly more than soliloquies. Mr. Huntington did somehow succeed in delaying for a number of years the enforcement of the Treasury's claims. However dangerous the plutocratic control of newspapers for sordid private ends may be, their control by demagogues for ambitious, selfish ends is an equally apparent evil. The people know, with unerring instinct, when a newspaper is devoted to private rather than to public interests; and their refusal to buy it limits its capacity for harm. But when a demagogic agitator appeals to "the masses" against "the classes" and poses as the ardent friend of the people against their "oppressors," assailing law and order and property as a means of gaining followers among the discontented and unthinking, the newspaper becomes a dangerous power for evil.

Commercialism has a legitimate place in a newspaper, namely, in the business office. The more successful a newspaper is commercially the better for its moral side. The more prosperous it is the more independent it can afford to be, the higher salaries it can pay to editors and reporters, the less subject it will be to temptation, the better it can stand losses for the sake of principle and conviction. But commercialism, which is proper and necessary in the business office, becomes a degradation and a danger when it invades the editorial rooms. Once let the public come to regard the press as exclusively a commercial business and there is an end of its moral power. Influence cannot exist without public confidence. And that confidence must have a human basis. It must rest in the end on the character of the journalist. The editor, the real "journalist" of the future, must be a man of such known integrity that he will be above the suspicion of writing or editing against his convictions. He must be known as one who would resign rather than sacrifice his principles to any business interest. It would be well if the editor of every newspaper were also its proprietor, but every editor can be at least the proprietor of himself. If he cannot keep the paper from degrading itself he can refuse to be a party to the degradation.

By far the larger part of the American press is honest, although partisan. It means to do right; it would like to know how. To strengthen its resolution and give to its wisdom the indispensable basis of knowledge and independent character is the object of training in journalism.

"I know but two ways by which society can be governed : the one is by Public Opinion, the other by the Sword."—MACAULAY.

The March of Progress

In an interesting review of its seventy years of life the New York *Sun* estimated the total circulation of the six morning papers existing in New York at its birth at 18,000 copies a day. Since then four of these six journals have died and the *Tribune, Times, Herald* and *World* have been born.

To-day the New York morning papers alone print more than a million copies of every issue. At least 1,500,000 copies more are added every working-day by the evening papers, which seventy years ago did not exist. In other words, for every New York newspaper sold in 1833 140 are sold now to fourteen times as many people. Where there used to be nearly three families to every newspaper there are now over three newspapers to every family.

There are men now living whose memories can bridge that gap of seventy years. In 1833 Andrew Jackson was President. The entire United States had less than the present population of the States of New York and Pennsylvania, and far less wealth than is concentrated to-day within half a mile of Trinity Church. There was not an American settlement west of the Missouri, and a few cabins were the only marks of civilization on the site of Chicago. New York City was smaller than Detroit is now. Washington was a swamp in which coaches were mired down and abandoned on Pennsylvania Avenue, and cows grazed on the site of the British Embassy. A generation had passed since Jackson had resigned his seat in the Senate because it took him nearly six weeks to make the journey between Philadelphia, then the capital, and his home,—a longer time than it has taken within the past year to girdle the globe,—but there were yet Senators who found the trip to Washington not much shorter. Still there were steamboats on the navigable rivers, and stage-coaches drawn over rails by steam-engines had just begun to astonish the inhabitants of a few favored localities. The horse was still the usual motor for high-speed traffic and the ox or the mule the customary freight-engine. " De Witt Clinton's ditch " across the State of New York was the commercial marvel of the age. The people of Virginia were strangers to the people of Pennsylvania, and the journey from Philadelphia to Pittsburg was longer and vastly more arduous than the journey now from Boston to the City of Mexico. The farmer reaped his grain with a scythe and cradle and threshed it with a flail or under the feet of horses. Whale-oil lamps glimmered feebly through the darkness of the city streets. Nails were made by hand on the blacksmith's forge. In the country a calico gown was a luxury, to be worn on state occasions. Colleges were few and puny. Harvard, the most ambitious of them all, was a high school in which a few professors taught Latin, Greek, moral philosophy and a little mathematics, leading in most cases to a course in theology. There was not a single real university in America. There were no great libraries.

In the best presses of that day, and for many years after, it was necessary to feed the paper by hand, one sheet at a time, print it on one side, and then feed it again and print it on the other. All the presses then in existence would not have been able to print a single edition of a leading New York newspaper of our time such as whirls between the cylinders of a Hoe machine from endless rolls of paper at the speed of the Niagara rapids. All the paper-mills then in the country could not have met the demands of such a journal for white paper. All the news-gathering agencies in the world would have hopelessly broken down in the attempt to provide even a fraction of its present daily supply of information. Had any one suggested then that children were already born who would be still living and reading when news would be flashed from Tokyo to New York by lightning and printed before it happened ; who would see on the same page despatches of the same date from India, from Siberia, from Australia, from Corea, and from the sources of the Nile ; that one of them in Boston could talk with his own voice to another in Omaha; that they would see newspapers printed on ships on the Atlantic containing news shot on invisible waves over a thousand miles of ocean, and that they could take breakfast in New York and dine in London a week later, he would have been treated as an eccentric "visionary."

So much for the seventy years upon which the old man can look back—what of the seventy years to which the boy can look forward?

The population of the Republic is still increasing at a rate that is more than equivalent to annexing a Canada every four years. New York promises to displace London in twenty or thirty years as the first city of the world. Nearly a million immigrants landed last year—the greatest human flood in all modern history. Electric trains have already been driven at a hundred and fifty miles an hour—as great an advance on the ordinary express train of 1904 as that has been on the stage-coach of 1833. Wireless telegraphy is in its feeble infancy and radium is hinting of things unsuspected. The nations are drawing together. The International Postal Union and international conventions on copyrights, tariffs, arbitration and other matters of common concern are teaching the people that it is as easy to co-operate as to quarrel. At the smallest rate of increase we have ever known in any census period the population of the United States would not be less than 290,000,000 in seventy years from now. Even allowing for any reasonable decline in the rate of growth it can hardly fall below 200,000,000.

We are embarked, whether we like it or not, upon a revolution in thought and life. Progress is sweeping forward with accelerating force, outstripping in decades the advance of former centuries and millenniums. All professions, all occupations but one, are keeping step with this majestic march. Its inspiration has fired all ranks of the marching army—or must we except the standard-bearers ? The self-constituted leaders and enlighteners of the people—what are they doing ? Standing still, lost in self-admiration, while the hosts march by ? Are they even doing as well as that ? Is it not a fact that the editors of seventy years ago were, as a rule, better informed in law, politics, government and history than those of to-day ? The statesmen and lawyers and political students who used to do editorial work for ambition or intellectual pleasure have ceased to frequent the news-paper offices. There is no trade so humble that it is not de-veloping a standard of progressive competence based on thorough training. For the more intellectual professions—law, medicine, art, architecture, music, engineering in all its varied branches—the years of preparation are stretching over ever-lengthening periods.

Is the most exacting profession of all—the one that requires the widest and the deepest knowledge and the firmest foundations of character—to be left entirely to the chances of self-education ? Is the man who is everybody's critic and teacher the only one who does himself not need to be taught ?

" He (Gladstone) was never very ready to talk about himself, but when asked what he regarded as his master secret, he always said, ' Concentration.' Steady practice of instant, fixed, effectual attention. . . ."—JOHN MORLEY.

What Should Be Taught— and How ?

Style.—Everybody says that a college of journalism must teach good English style. But what is a good style and how shall it be taught ?

The importance and the rarity of a really good English style are so great that, to my own mind, this college will be worth all it costs if it shall succeed only in teaching the future gen-erations of journalists what a wonderful art Style is and how to perfect themselves in it.

"The style is the man," said Buffon ; by which he obviously meant that the best thing in any man's writing is that which is individual—giving his own thought in his own way. But the important thing is to develop the style that is the man in a manner to make it conform to the requisites of the best newspaper writing, namely, accuracy, clearness, terseness and forcefulness.

The literary art is in general very inadequately taught and very little appreciated in this country. No artist aspires to fame without a knowledge of form and color and drawing. But one has only to read the newspapers and the books without number issued from the press to perceive that many authors audaciously begin their careers without having learned to write.

In no profession is the art of writing more important than in journalism, which is daily turning out a literature—ephemeral, it is true, and in great part bad, but still the literature of the millions. Yet one style will not answer the manifold requirements of a newspaper. There must be a different style for each kind of work—polemical, descriptive, analytical, literary, satirical, expository, critical, narrative—and the mind of the editor, like a trained musical ear, must be able to detect every note out of place. An argumentative editorial on the tariff must not be written in the vein that would be appropriate to a pathetic description of a mother's search for a lost child, nor must a satirical dissection of a politician resemble a report of a bankruptcy case.

But through all the varied styles fit for use in a newspaper there runs one common feature—public interest. Whether the subject he touches be profound or trivial, the journalist must not be dull nor involved nor hard to understand. He must know exactly what he wants to say, how to say it and—when to stop. He must have a Gallic lucidity and precision.

He must have the critical faculty, for all newspaper work involves criticism and analysis. The journalist criticises everything under the sun ; his eye is always at the mental microscope and his hand on the dissecting-knife.

Acute journalists gradually fashion their own styles through observation and practice. They can never be relieved of that necessity by any attempt to fit a ready-made style to them ; but may they not be helped by a course of instruction systematically explaining what journalism requires, with illustrations of good and bad work ?

"Honest and independent journalism is the mightiest force evolved by modern civilization. With **The Law** all its faults—and what human institution is faultless ?—it is indispensable to the life of a free people. The frontiers of the constitutional privilege of the press are as wide as human thought, and it is one of the glories of our country that its journalism as a whole is incorrupt, fearless and patriotic. It is the never-sleeping enemy of bigotry, sectionalism, ignorance and crime. It deserves the freedom which our fathers gave it. It has justified itself."—ALTON B. PARKER, *Chief Judge of the New York Court of Appeals.*

Everybody says that Law must be taught. Assuredly !—but how ?

There are manifold branches of the law. International law, constitutional interpretation, the law of corporations, of contracts, of real estate, wills, patents, divorce, the criminal law and a score of other important subjects, each command the almost undivided attention of legal experts who have practically become specialists.

To attempt the mastery of all phases of the law as taught in a law school would be impossible for a student of journalism. Nor is it necessary. Here, again, the fundamental idea underlying the entire scheme of this college, of *specializing the instruction,* is seen to be essential. The regular student of law must learn not merely the principles but the practice and precedents of his profession. But the journalist needs to know only the principles and theories of law and so much of their application as relates directly to the rights and the welfare of the public. The art of selection must be employed in separating the essential and the practical from the non-essential and the impractical.

Take the question of franchises, which has become so important to municipalities and to the country at large. Would not a series of special lectures, prepared by a competent jurist, instruct those who aim to become teachers and guardians of the people as to the nature and proper limitations of public franchises? A clear definition of the nature and responsibilities of a "common carrier" and of the reservations and conditions which it is right to impose upon corporations that seek the use of public property, like the streets of a city, for private gain, would be of great advantage to those who will be called upon to protect the public interests in the future.

There is much in the papers—and a good deal, it must be confessed, that is either ignorant or demagogic, or both—in denunciation of monopolies. How many know the fundamental fact that oppressive monopolies are abhorrent to the common law, which we inherited from England? How many know the difference between common law and statute law? President Cleveland, President Roosevelt and even the astute Mr. Olney thought a constitutional amendment necessary to enable Congress to forbid and punish "trusts, monopolies or other conspiracies in restraint of trade." But the Supreme Court has frequently decided, and has just reaffirmed the truth I have maintained for fourteen years, that under the common law all these combinations are unlawful and subject to the restraint of Congress under the Constitution.

The relations of capital and labor, which present one of the greatest problems before us as a nation and one filled with potentialities of the gravest danger, and the ownership or regulation of public utilities by municipalities or by the nation, both involve many strictly legal or constitutional points. The discussion of these questions in the press is too commonly partisan, superficial or demagogic. Would it not be of great advantage to the press and the public if journalists were instructed in the basic principles of law and equity in these matters? Is it not entirely practicable to teach them the legal meaning of such phases as "eminent domain," "vested rights," "the public welfare" (as used in the Constitution), "corporate privileges," and the like?

The writ of injunction,—or "government by injunction" as it has been mischievously called,—would it not be enlightening and useful if a great jurist like Justice Brewer or James C. Carter or Joseph Choate were to give to the students in the College of Journalism a history of this writ and a dispassionate account of its uses and necessity and possible limitations in a free government?

And so of divorce—the press teems with scandals arising from the too easy sundering of marriage ties. Clergymen deplore its evils, moralists suggest impossible remedies, legislators meddle only to muddle. Would it not conduce to the enactment of a national divorce law, uniform and stringent, if the journalists of the future were impressed with the anomaly of forty-five separate and often conflicting laws of marriage and divorce in this indissoluble Union?

The fundamental things—the settled principles of law—that touch closely the life and the welfare of the people can surely be taught in a series of lectures by eminent lawyers, aided by the standard text-books. Nearly forty years ago, preparatory to my admission to the bar in St. Louis, I not only read but *studied* Blackstone; and I have never seen the day in my whole journalistic experience when I did not feel thankful for what I then learned of the *principles* of law.

A carefully specialized course of study adapted to teach the student of journalism what he needs to know, and omitting the things that are not required by one who has no intention of practising law, will, it seems to me, prove to be not only wholly practicable, but in the highest degree useful. No subject is more important, for Law is the basis of Civilization, the regulator of Liberty, the safeguard of Order, the formal expression of a nation's ideas of Justice—and Justice is the supreme test of any and all government.

Ethics Everybody says that ethics should be taught. But how?

I have expressed myself poorly indeed if I have not made it clear that here is the heart of the whole matter.

Without high ethical ideals a newspaper, however amusing and prosperous, not only is stripped of its splendid possibilities of public service, but may become a positive danger to the community. There will naturally be a course in ethics, but training in ethical principles must not be confined to that. It must pervade all the courses. Ideals, character, professional standards not to be infringed without shame, a sense of honor which, as Burke said of the totally undeserving French noblesse, feels a stain like a wound: these will be the motif of the whole institution, never forgotten even in its most practical work.

News is important — it is the very life of a paper. But what is life without character? What is the life of a nation or of an individual without honor, without heart and soul?

Above knowledge, above news, above intelligence, the heart and soul of a paper lie in its moral sense, in its courage, its integrity, its humanity, its sympathy for the oppressed, its independence, its devotion to the public welfare, its anxiety to render public service.

Without these there may be clever journalists, but never a truly great or honorable one.

Everybody says a journalist must study literature. True — Literature but how ? A college course is too short to allow even the barest introduction to all the great works with which a newspaper writer ought to be familiar. But it can make a beginning, which can be intelligent and thorough as far as it goes. The student would have time enough to become intimately acquainted with a few of the masterpieces whose web of imagery and allusion has become part of the texture of English style.

Perhaps I may take it for granted that in this course particular attention will be paid to the literature of politics, from Plato to Burke, from the letters of Junius to Hamilton's famous Federalist letters, and from Jefferson to Lincoln.

Everybody says that a journalist ought to be taught the im- Truth and portance of truth and accuracy. But how ? Accuracy

Journalism implies the duty and art of omniscience. A newspaper never admits that there is anything it does not know. But while the newspaper may know everything, the man who helps to make it does not, and owing to the limited capacity of the human brain he never can.

More important, therefore, than filling him up with facts that can never reach the measure of his needs is his instruction in the art of finding things when they are required. Does a reader ask how many national bank-notes were outstanding in 1867 ? The editor may not know, but by turning to the report of the Comptroller of the Currency he can find out, and then the paper knows.

The library of reference is the editor's best friend, and the art of going at once to the proper source for any needed piece of information is one of the most useful arts a journalist can possibly acquire. And is not this something that could easily be taught in a class-room ?

The bibliography of books of reference, with instruction in the art of finding data with speed and precision, would make a well-defined college course. There is always some best source for every kind of information — some original source from which the facts trickle through all sorts of media and finally reach the public at second, third or fourth hand.

To know these sources of exact knowledge, to be able to put one's hand on them instantly, and so to be able to state facts with absolute confidence in their accuracy—could there be any more useful equipment for a journalist ?

History " He alone reads history aright who, observing how powerfully circumstances influence the feelings and opinions of men, how often virtues pass into vices and paradoxes into axioms, learns to distinguish what is accidental and transitory in human nature from what is essential and immutable."—MACAULAY.

Everybody says that a school of journalism must teach history. But how ? The world's historical records fill thousands of volumes. The utmost that any scholar can do in a whole lifetime is to dip into this mass of material here and there and take out something that he particularly wants. But the average college class is composed of young men with all kinds of purposes, and therefore with all kinds of wants, and these young men must all be taught together. Therefore the professor, perforce, prepares for them a neutral course.

Now let us suppose that instead of lecturing for the general student in a general way a professor of history should concentrate sharply upon the special object of the journalist, upon the special, separate needs of his training. Might he not then find time to throw light upon such subjects as these :

The history of politics. (" History," said Seeley, " is past politics and politics is future history.")

The growth and development of free institutions and the causes of their decay.

Revolutions, reforms and changes of government.

The influence of public opinion upon all progress.

Legislation.

Taxation.

Moral movements.

Slavery and war.

Conflicts between capital and labor.

The history of colonization, illuminating American policy by European experience.

The history of journalism.

Of course, in this review general history would be lightly touched, English history more thoroughly, and American history would have several times as much attention as all the rest combined. And through all its phases would run the idea of progress, especially the progress of justice, of civilization, of humanity, of public opinion and of the democratic idea and ideal.

Everybody says that a college of journalism should teach Sociology sociology. But how?

Vague and almost formless as this science is, it is full of the raw material of the newspaper. Charles Booth's monumental seventeen volumes on the life and labor of the people of London, with its maps showing block by block where the thrifty workers congregate and where live the submerged tenth,— where dens of vice elbow schools and where the saloon crowds upon the tenement,— are the last condensation of a hundred years of reporting. Sociology, the science of the life of man in society, is the systematization of facts which it is the daily business of the journalist to collect.

The chief difficulty in teaching this science is that it is so very broad — like a river in flood, without any definite channel. But

56

a professor who knows what to leave out can frame a course, theoretical and practical, that will be one of the best possible introductions to newspaper work.

Economics Everybody says that a college of journalism should teach economics. But how?

May I not say with confidence that it should not confine itself to the old, arid, abstract political economy, but should deal with the new play of industrial and commercial forces that is transforming modern society?

The relations between capital and labor, for instance. Can a journalist be too well informed about that? There are things here of which the old economists, with their "haggling of the market" and their "natural laws of wages," never dreamed.

The Enemies of the Republic There are dangers ahead for the Republic. The demagogue is in the land. He is trying to array society into two camps. There is a new irrepressible conflict which it is folly to ignore. The stupendous growth of corporate power; the enormous increase in individual fortunes, combined to control railroad systems and industries, defiant of law and destructive of competition; the growing inequalities in life, in station and in opportunity; the practical disfranchisement of many millions of citizens equal under the Constitution; the enormous mass of illiteracy and political unfitness in the Southern States; the intensified antagonism of labor against corporate capital, of employees against employers, the growth of corruption in cities — are problems which will tax the wisdom of our statesmen and the serene self-confidence of our people.

This confidence would be sublime if it were not blind! What reason have we for thinking that our Government is exempt from the mutations of history? Is not, in fact, our Republic liable to popular passion, sitting as it does in a glass house, subject to the conflicts, the disturbances and the possible reactions of elections every two and four years ?

A change of 25,000 votes in certain close States in 1896 would have put Mr. Bryan into the White House and have given him the appointment of three Supreme Court justices. With growing discontent, with appeals to ignorance by some newspapers, powerfully assisted by the proceedings of some financiers who act on the principle, "after us the deluge," who can be so dense as not to see the certainty of popular reaction against the money power, the rich, especially in hard times? Is it inconceivable that an element that could command over six million votes in 1896 might, under other conditions, secure twenty-five thousand more? Who can be so overconfident of the future as not to see that the very fire of liberty, maintained by universal suffrage, brings danger every two years or every four years, unless that liberty be regulated by law, order, intelligence and self-control?

And can we ignore the growing power and intelligence of organized labor in any course of economic study? Not only do the labor-unions represent organized hostility to organized capital, but they now display this very remarkable development — that they do not represent poor labor, destitute labor, as they formerly did and are supposed by some still to do, but what may fairly be called semi-capitalistic labor. Is it not most significant, that after a six months' strike in the anthracite regions, during which the idle miners were reported to have drawn a million dollars from the funds of their union, that union still has, on the authority of Mr. John Mitchell, approximately another million dollars in its treasury? The laborers, in fact, have become semi-capitalists through organization. When they are armed with such a weapon, with the power of co-operation, with a strong leader, and with at least a million of votes for which the politicians of both parties are

58

bidding, are there not sufficient possibilities to make the situation worth the study of men who assume to be popular teachers?

And Socialism!—a new economics in itself—treated as beyond the pale of respectable discussion a few years ago and now in principle actually triumphant in Germany, France, and even in so conservative a country as England,—whose bill for the purchase and distribution of landed estates in Ireland is the essence of state Socialism,—what of that? The German socialists openly refuse to be considered simply as a political party, accepting the present situation and trying to improve existing institutions from within. They proclaim their purpose as distinctly revolutionary.

We have socialistic beginnings in America, such as demands for the Government ownership of mines and railroads and a pension roll on which we have spent three thousand million dollars since the civil war, and to which, already containing a million names, 300,000 new names have just been added by an act of Executive usurpation. But our Socialism has no leaders like Jaurès and Bebel—two of the greatest intellects in Europe.

How soon shall we have two such men in America—not gifted merely with Mr. Bryan's talent for oratory, but with sound judgment, with stable character, and with sincerity of purpose that would give them a hold on the people not to be obtained except through that confidence which only such sincerity of character and soundness of judgment breed?

Arbitration And what are we to say of arbitration, that great engine of civilization, belonging equally to economics and to politics, and perhaps to ethics, which is daily proving its value as a substitute for disturbances, disorder, riot and war? The very act of submitting a dispute to arbitration proves that there is something to be said on both sides. The men who arrogantly issue demands for which they offer no reason but simple power have "nothing to arbitrate." Before an arbitration tribunal questions are discussed on their merits. Appeals to prejudice, to class or national animosities, to cynical self-interest, are dropped. Every such hearing is a lesson in order and civilization.

There is always a tendency on the part of the weaker side to ask for arbitration and on that of the stronger to refuse it. Here is the opportunity of the press to bring its moral force into the dispute and overcome the obstinacy of brute strength by the pressure of public opinion.

The literature of arbitration is already immense. The workings of experiments in compulsory arbitration, of boards of conciliation, of permanent State arbitration tribunals, of standing arbitration agreements between labor-unions and employers, and of the long line of international settlements leading up to the establishment of the world's court of arbitration at The Hague, would furnish material in themselves for a full and most valuable course of study for a journalist.

Everybody says that statistics should be taught. But how? **Statistics**

Statistics are not simply figures. It is said that nothing lies like figures—except facts. You want statistics to tell you the truth. You can find truth there if you know how to get at it, and romance, human interest, humor and fascinating revelations as well. The journalist must know how to find all these things—truth, of course, first. His figures must bear examination. It is much better to understate than to overstate his case, so that his critics and not himself may be put to confusion when they challenge him to verify his comparisons.

He must not read his statistics blindly; he must be able to test them by knowledge and by common sense. He must always be on the alert to discover how far they can actually be trusted—and what they really mean. The analysis of statistics to get at the essential truth of them has become a well-developed science whose principles are systematically taught. And what a fascinating science it is! What romance can equal the facts of our national growth?

Is it not a stupendous fact that there are 204,000 miles of railroad in the United States (more than in the whole of Europe), owned by companies having a total capitalization of more than $14,000,000,000, par value, affording livelihood to 5,000,000 of persons (employees and their families), and distributing $178,-000,000 in dividends to owners and $610,713,701 in wages?

The flow of our exports,—over three thousand millions above imports in seven years,—does not the imagination see in these figures the whole story of the recent forward rush of American industry—the "American invasion" of Europe and the homeward flight of securities? And then, are there not interesting reflections in the fact that we have spent almost exactly the same amount in pensions in the past thirty years? What a tribute to our institutions—what hope for the future—in the fact that 18,000,000 pupils are attending school or college! And immigration,—more than 20,000,000 since 1820; nearly a million arrivals last year—a New Zealand swallowed in a year, an Australia in four years,—surely it looks as if Europe were being transplanted bodily to America. But when we remember that the natural increase of the population of Europe is about four millions a year we may feel reasonably sure that the old continent will always have a few people left.

Modern Languages Everybody says a school of journalism should teach modern languages. But which?

It cannot treat them as a luxurious culture subject or as a mental discipline. It must regard each foreign language as a tool —a key with which to unlock the life, the literature, the morals and the manners of the people that use it. "He who knows no other tongue," said Goethe, "knows little of his own." And every additional tongue he can master is a new asset for the journalist. The special advantage of French is on the side of style. Order, precision, lucidity, artistic form, are all French characteristics, of especial value to the journalist.

An advantage of German is that it is, above all others, the language of translations. With that you have a key to everything else. Everything of importance in every other language, ancient or modern, has been translated into German, and translated wonderfully well. How much can be done in two or three years in the teaching of one or more modern languages as a part of that special course is a matter for the Advisory Board and the college authorities to consider.

Everybody says that physical science should be taught. But how ? **Physical Science**

Even when Pope said, " The proper study of mankind is man," there were some things outside of himself that were worth a little of a philosopher's attention. But in this age it is impossible to make even a pretence of intelligence, not to speak of filling the post of a public teacher without, at least, a little scientific knowledge.

The journalist need not be a specialist in science ; he need not even follow the ordinary scientific courses at college, which are too choked with small details to answer his needs. But ought he not to have some bold outlines of the principles of physics, chemistry, biology and astronomy, in the light of the latest discoveries, with such an introduction to the best authorities on these subjects as would enable him to follow them to any further extent by himself?

Everybody says that in the training of a journalist the current newspapers must be studied. But how ? **The Study of Newspapers**

Suppose the managing or chief editor of a great daily, moved by a generous zeal for his profession, should give several hours to a thorough study of the newspapers of the current day. Then let us imagine him saying to a class : " Here is the best and here is the worst story of the day " — and telling why. " Here is the wrong of the day; here is the injustice that needs to be righted ; here is the best editorial ; here is a brilliant paragraph ; here is a bit of sentimental trash ; here is a superb ' beat '; here is a scandalous ' fake ' for which the perpetrator ought to go to Sing Sing ; here is a grossly inaccurate and misleading headline ; here is an example of crass ignorance of foreign politics ; here is something ' crammed ' from an almanac by a man who does not know the meaning of figures when he sees them."

If the editors of twenty of the foremost journals in the country should deliver such lectures in turn, " demonstrating " from the day's paper as the lecturer in a medical college does from the object of his clinic, could a young man worth his room in a newspaper office go through a year of their training without learning to see and to think ? Would not that course alone be a liberal education ?

The Power of Ideas

" Public opinion is at once the guide and the monitor of statesmen." —ERSKINE MAY.

Everybody says that journalistic ideas should be taught. But how ? — and by whom ?

Goethe said : " Everything has been thought of before, but the difficulty is to think of it again." If everything has been thought of before, it can all be recalled and set down in order. You can make a list of all the important ideas that brought honor and success in journalism in the last twenty years. Would it be possible for anybody, unless he were a fool, to survey for three hundred days in the year a procession of ideas on which successful and respectable newspapers had been founded and maintained without absorbing, digesting, assimilating and unconsciously taking into his brain thought which he could apply to his own needs ?

Fools have had no place in my plans for a college of journalism. They belong with the journalists who are " born, not made."

To think rightly, to think instantly, to think incessantly, to think intensely, to seize opportunities when others let them go by —this is the secret of success in journalism. To teach this is twenty times more important than to teach Latin or Greek.

Napoleon said that every battle depended upon one thought, but that one thought, though seeming to be a sudden inspiration, was the result of a whole life of thinking and experience.

Thought is the only power that has no limits. You may say of a steam boiler : " This will develop a thousand horse-power," but who can say where the influence of a thought will stop ?

The French Revolution sprang from the thought of a few men. Voltaire, Rousseau and the Encyclopædists said that the idea of the people belonging to the King by divine right was preposterous ; that the people belonged to themselves. This thought-germ floated in the air ; the American Revolution stimulated it, and suddenly the awakened people made the thought a deed.

An old thought applied to a new situation is new. Robespierre spoke of "government of the people, by the people, for the people" long before Lincoln was born. Yet who remembers Robespierre in connection with that phrase which Lincoln re-created and immortalized ?

Before the days of railroads, of telegraphs or of great industrial and commercial combinations a thinker in France attacked corporations as a danger to the state, because, having no souls, they were destitute of that sense of pride and personal responsibility, of individual shame and honor, without which good citizenship is impossible. It was the idea of Helvetius that devotion to the state is the first duty of patriotism. In his day that idea seemed purely theoretical; corporations were not then really formidable. But the thought was sound and the time has come when it is practical.

"There is nothing new under the sun." Mr. Bryan's idea of scaling down debts by law is as old as social discontent. If he had read history attentively he would not have taken himself so seriously as an agitator. His scheme was tried by Lycurgus, by Solon, by the Gracchi; it was part of the programme of Catiline. Even the method of doing it, by depreciating the value of the coinage, was applied repeatedly by European kings in the Middle Ages and later.

None of us can hope to be original. We simply take from the great stock of old thoughts what suits our purpose, and it depends upon ourselves and our training whether we select the good or the bad.

Principles of Journalism Everybody says that we should teach the principles and methods of journalism. But how?

Well, it seems impossible to do so without lectures explaining the subject in a systematic way. But would not still more be gained from the actual preparation by the students of a newspaper to be printed, perhaps, once a week at first, by means of a press and plant, for which I have provided, in the college building?

Such a paper would give practice in all branches of newspaper work—editing, reporting, criticising, copy-reading, proof-reading, making-up—everything, in short, that a young man ought to be able to do before he ventures to undertake the work of a journalist. It would be under the supervision of a professor who would not only wield the pencil as ruthlessly as a real editor does, but would also do what the real editor has no time to do—tell why he did it. Sometimes all the students might be asked to write editorials on the same subject, and the best one could be printed, with an explanation of the reasons for its selection.

If the ablest twenty editors in the country, or in the East, or in New York, were to consent to take turns once or twice a year in analyzing and criticising the paper so produced and the New York dailies, putting their best thought and experience into the task, the students would have the benefit, not of one mind, but of twenty, and these the best in the profession. Would not editors in sympathy with the plan do this much as a matter of pride, of honor? By such practice, under such expert criticism, the journalist would be trained for work, as the young officer is trained for war by military manœuvres.

But the object of the course would be always to make real editors, to develop right thinking—to teach the student that what makes a newspaper is not type, nor presses, nor advertising, but brains, conscience, character working out into public service.

But I must stop—and should perhaps apologize for the interminable length of this paper, which has exceeded all reasonable bounds. The writing of it has convinced me that the two years' course of study suggested for the College of Journalism would be altogether too short—for, after all, we have not yet said anything about news. *Finale— The News*

It is not that I underestimate its value. News is the life of a paper. It is perennially changing—more varied than any kaleidoscope, bringing every day some new surprise, some new sensation —always the unexpected.

But I have no time to treat the subject adequately, and ought to confess that the editorial discussion of politics and public questions has ever been the matter of deepest personal interest to me.

News is very interesting, but there are others who no doubt

will take care of it better than I. Give me a news editor who has been well grounded, who has the foundations of accuracy, love of truth and an instinct for the public service, and there will be no trouble about his gathering the news.

Public Service the Supreme End

" What are great gifts but the correlative of great work ? We are not born for ourselves but for our kind, for our neighbors, for our country."—CARDINAL NEWMAN.

It has been said by some that my object in founding the College of Journalism was to help young men who wish to make this their vocation. Others have commended it as an effort to raise journalism to its real rank as one of the learned professions. This is true. But while it is a great pleasure to feel that a large number of young men will be helped to a better start in life by means of this college, this is not my primary object. Neither is the elevation of the profession which I love so much and regard so highly. In all my planning the chief end I had in view was the welfare of the Republic. It will be the object of the college to make better journalists, who will make better newspapers, which will better serve the public. It will impart knowledge—not for its own sake, but to be used for the public service. It will try to develop character, but even that will be only a means to the one supreme end—the public good. We are facing that hitherto unheard-of portent—an innumerable, world-wide, educated and self-conscious democracy. The little revolutions of the past have been effected by a few leaders working upon an ignorant populace, conscious only of vague feelings of discontent. Now the masses read. They know their grievances and their power. They discuss in New York the position of labor in Berlin and in Sydney. Capital, too, is developing a world-wide class feeling. It likewise has learned the power of co-operation.

What will be the state of society and of politics in this Republic seventy years hence, when some of the children now in school

46

will be still living ? Shall we preserve the government of the Constitution, the equality of all citizens before the law and the purity of justice—or shall we have the government of either money or the mob ?

The answers to these questions will depend largely upon the kind of instruction the people of that day draw from their news-papers—the text-books, the orators, the preachers of the masses.

I have said so much of the need for improvement in journalism that to avoid misconception I must put on record my appreciation of the really admirable work so many newspaper men are doing already. The competent editorial writer, for instance—how much sound information he furnishes every day ! How generally just his judgments are, and how prompt his decisions ! Unknown to the people he serves, he is in close sympathy with their feelings and aspirations, and when left to himself and unhampered by party prejudices he generally interprets their thought as they would wish to express it themselves.

It is not too much to say that the press is the only great organ-ized force which is actively and as a body upholding the standard of civic righteousness. There are many political reformers among the clergy, but the pulpit as an institution is concerned with the Kingdom of Heaven, not with the Republic of America. There are many public-spirited lawyers, but the bar as a profession works for its retainers, and no law-defying trust ever came to grief from a dearth of legal talent to serve it. Physicians work for their pa-tients and architects for their patrons. The press alone makes the public interests its own. "What is everybody's business is no-body's business"—except the journalist's ; it is his by adoption. But for his care almost every reform would fall stillborn. He holds officials to their duty. He exposes secret schemes of plunder. He promotes every hopeful plan of progress. Without him public opinion would be shapeless and dumb. He brings all classes, all professions together, and teaches them to act in concert on the basis of their common citizenship.

The Greeks thought that no republic could be successfully governed if it were too large for all the citizens to come together in one place. The Athenian democracy could all meet in the popular assembly. There public opinion was made, and accordingly as the people listened to a Pericles or to a Cleon the state flourished or declined. The orator that reaches the American democracy is the newspaper. It alone makes it possible to keep the political blood in healthful circulation in the veins of a continental republic. We have—it is unfortunately true—a few newspapers which advocate dangerous fallacies and falsehoods, appealing to ignorance, to partisanship, to passion, to popular prejudice, to poverty, to hatred of the rich, to socialism, sowing the seeds of discontent—eventually sure, if unchecked, to produce lawlessness and bloodshed. Virtue, said Montesquieu, is the principle of a republic, and therefore a republic, which in its purity is the most desirable of all forms of government, is the hardest of all to preserve. For there is nothing more subject to decay than virtue.

Our Republic and its press will rise or fall together. An able, disinterested, public-spirited press, with trained intelligence to know the right and courage to do it, can preserve that public virtue without which popular government is a sham and a mockery. A cynical, mercenary, demagogic, corrupt press will produce in time a people as base as itself. The power to mould the future of the Republic will be in the hands of the journalists of future generations. This is why I urge my colleagues to aid this important experiment. Upon their generous aid and cooperation the ultimate success of the project must depend.

JOSEPH PULITZER.

The Power of Public Opinion[1]

In attempting to estimate the sources, the power and limitations of public opinion it is necessary first to determine what public opinion is. Webster defines private opinion as "the judgment or sentiment which the mind forms of persons or things." More broadly, it may be defined as a conviction based on evidence, an assent secured by argument, or a view acquired, perhaps unconsciously, through the reading habit. Public opinion may be described as the aggregate of private opinion. It is what the mass or the majority believes or feels. A popular government is government by public opinion expressed in elections and formulated in statutes. Public opinion as it regulates the conduct of a community is an unwritten law—a dominant sentiment representing a common agreement or code of morals and manners.

History shows in nearly every age the force of public opinion. In the democratic communities of Greece the great orators Pericles, Demosthenes and their disciples influenced events through their appeals to the people. In Rome public opinion was potent alike under the republic and the empire. Mark Antony's harangue, stirring up civil war, was to the populace. It

Examples in History

---

[1] Reprinted by permission from the *Encyclopedia Americana.*

was not until the Reformation in England had finally gained over public opinion that it became firmly established. It was responsible for the civil war, for the reaction in favor of Charles II., for the expulsion of James II., his brother and successor, for the selection of William of Orange and the introduction of the Hanoverian dynasty. Public opinion in England forced upon successive Cabinets the necessity for reform of the franchise and of the corn laws. Public opinion directed the Declaration of Independence in this country and sustained the long war for freedom. Public opinion was the prime cause of the unification and emancipation of Italy and of the consolidation of the German Empire. Public opinion inspired and carried through the successive revolutions in France in 1789, 1830, 1848 and 1870. In the latter year the fall of the empire and the establishment of the republic was effected by a proclamation in the streets and without the shedding of blood.

In every state whose system of government is in essence democratic no change of dynasty, of administration, of constitution, can be effected that is not directly caused by the operation of public opinion. In modern government public opinion is effective in exact ratio to the freedom of the people. Jefferson called public opinion "that lord of the universe." But it is not lord in Russia, for it is fettered there. Wendell Phillips, at the height of the anti-slavery agitation in New England, said if he lived in Russia he should be an Anarchist, because in that land there was "no free press, no Faneuil Hall, no ballot-box." But in a country like ours, where, as General Grant said, "the will of the people is the law of the land," it is highly important to know what are the creative causes of public opinion. When is it to be followed and when opposed ? What is the best method of influencing it ? How shall it be directed to produce practical results ?

Public opinion as a moral and political force finds its inspiration and its expression in the press and on the platform. Gutenberg was the founder of modern public opinion. The printing press was a most important factor in disseminating the religious views advocated by the Reformers and in thus fashioning a supporting public opinion. The spoken words of Luther reached only the few; printed they reached the many. Thousands of tracts and pamphlets were scattered throughout Germany, carrying the thought-germs of the new religious ideas. With the advent of the newspaper there began to be felt in the world a new power— "the mightiest ever known for the creation, development and direction of the greatest of modern forces—majority public opinion."

The astute De Tocqueville said : "A newspaper can drop the same thought into a thousand minds at the same moment." But now one newspaper can drop the same thought into a million minds on the same day. In 1900, according to the census of that year, the 2,226 daily newspapers of this country had an aggregate circulation of 15,102,156 copies. The total circulation per issue of all newspapers and periodicals was 114,299,334, and the aggregate number of copies circulated in a year reached the almost inconceivable total of 8,168,148,749. Nearly one thousand of the principal daily papers of the country, with an aggregate circulation of more than 13,000,000, belong to one great news organization— the Associated Press of the United States. They receive the same despatches, covering every habitable quarter of the globe. The same facts, the same condensations of news and views, are "dropped into the mind" of these millions of readers on the same day.

This instantaneous and constant enlightenment of the people as to the affairs of our own country and of the world was what

The Press as Its Inspiration and Expression

the writer had in view in saying, ten years ago : "Publicity is the greatest moral factor and force in the universe." President Eliot of Harvard expressed the same view, seven years later, in saying : "Publicity is the great security for democracy, the best weapon against political, social, industrial or commercial wrong-doing, and in the long run the most trustworthy means of political and social progress." And Justice Brewer, of the United States Supreme Court, in a brief but pregnant statement on "the effect of a free press on American life," written for the New York *World,* spoke of the service of the press " in the evolution of the court of public opinion, that court mightier than any organized tribunal, at whose bar are judged all men, events and parties."

Is the Influence of the Press Declining ? It is sometimes said by superficial observers that the influence of the press is declining. How can it decline when its character has steadily improved and its aggregate circulation has enormously increased ? Have facts lost their power ? Does information no longer promote intelligence ? Are men less responsive than formerly to sound arguments and sensible appeals ? Thirty years ago an eminent bishop of the Episcopal Church said : " It is the press that creates public opinion. It is the grand fact of the hour that popular sentiment has been educated by the press up to the point of spurning party trammels and voting on principle."

If this were true in 1873 how much more universally true is it now ! Nearly every great newspaper in this country to-day is independent—financially and politically. The last six Presidential elections have been decided by the independent vote, led by the independent press.

The result of the municipal election in the city of New York in 1903, when the Tammany candidate for Mayor was elected by a plurality of 62,000, in spite of the practically united opposition of the press of the city, has been cited as evidence that the newspapers have not the influence commonly attributed to them. It is to be noted, however, that the Democratic majority was reduced one-half from that secured in the preceding year ; that in the city there are tens of thousands of illiterate voters who are not susceptible to the arguments or appeals of the press ; that an even greater number cannot read, and that a very large proportion of the total number of voters are impervious to argument in an election by reason of their ingrained but honest partisanship or by a selfish interest in the success of the ticket of their choice—as the saloon-keepers and their patrons, the law-breaking classes, the office-seekers, etc. That in a total vote of nearly 600,000, representing a normal Democratic majority of 120,000, a non-partisan ticket needed only 5 per cent. more of the vote to have triumphed is really a tribute to the influence of the press, particularly in the light of the strange mistake made in defying public opinion by strictly enforcing obsolete puritanical Sunday laws which the majority of the cosmopolitan people of the city regard as odious infringements of their personal liberty.

The journalist acts upon and through public opinion, and therefore, from his point of view, the development of public opinion is the central thread of history. It is inseparably connected with the growth of his own profession. History is filled with accounts of wars and their causes, but to the journalist the remarkable point in that relation is the fact that wars used to be made by individual caprice, while to-day no great duel between nations can be begun or carried on without the support of public opinion. For example, in 1870 Napoleon III. and King William were in legal theory the war lords of France and Prussia. Personally they both sincerely wanted peace, yet they could not have it. Bismarck wanted war, and he got it by manipulating public opinion, which was stronger than the monarchs. He

The Controlling Factor in National Affairs

excited the French by permitting the candidature of a Hohenzollern prince for the throne of Spain. Then that was withdrawn and Bismarck seemed checkmated. He and his associates of the Prussian war party, Moltke and Roon, were in despair, when Napoleon III. fatuously helped them by demanding an assurance that no Hohenzollern ever would accept the Spanish throne in the future. Benedetti, the French Ambassador, stopped King William on the Parade at Ems to urge this demand, and the King, losing patience, turned his back. The Parisian press raged at this "insult to France," while Bismarck, by some judicious alterations in the despatch in which the King had described this incident, made it appear that the French Government had insulted the Prussian sovereign, and the German press was ablaze. Public opinion was roused now in both countries, and two almost absolute monarchs were forced to yield to it and go to war against their own desires.

In Morley's "Life of Gladstone" it is recorded that Lord Aberdeen suffered "incessant self-reproach" for not having striven harder to prevent the Crimean war ; and he asked Mr. Gladstone, who was a member of his Cabinet, whether he did not think that he (Lord Aberdeen) "might withdraw from office when we came to the declaration of war," as "all along he had been acting against his feelings." Mr. Gladstone, though sympathizing with Lord Aberdeen's antipathy to any except defensive war, said of the war against Russia : "The government are certainly giving effect to the public opinion of the day."

Many honest Democrats in America, and even some Republicans, doubted the wisdom of opposing secession by war. At the time of his inauguration President Lincoln had no conception of the terrible task before him. He thought in his first call upon the nation for troops that he was going to suppress the rebellion in three months with 75,000 men—an incredible blunder when it is remembered that the total number of men engaged on the Union side during the four years of war became 2,772,408. The press did its duty in that time of danger and doubt. But suppose it had not; suppose it had left public opinion apathetic—would Lincoln have dared to enforce the draft? Would he have dared to call out half the men of military age in the North? Would he have ventured to issue the Emancipation Proclamation? Would he not have offered compromises and concessions for the sake of peace? The public opinion of the North carried on the war for the Union. Lincoln, great genius and matchless leader though he was, was its masterful instrument.

In surveying the growing power of public opinion the journalist must become impressed with a sense of the grave responsibility resting upon all who have any share in the guidance of that mighty force. If he have imagination enough to picture to himself the consequences of inciting national animosities—if he can track reckless words to the grim realities that follow them, on the battlefield and in widowed homes, must he not recoil with horror and indignation from wanton provocation to war?

President McKinley was opposed to the war with Spain and, mild-mannered as he was, resisted Congress and the popular sentiment as long as he dared. Yet in the end he had to yield his well-known and freely expressed convictions to the demand of the public and the press, while Congress "held a stop-watch" on him to see that the yielding was not delayed. A less striking but still significant example is the historic fact that Mr. McKinley, who as a Representative in Congress voted for the free and unlimited coinage of silver in 1877, became the candidate and champion of the gold standard party in 1896, owing to the change of public sentiment on this question in his own State and in the nation.

In our labor wars, too, public opinion presses with a force

that is not to be resisted. In the great coal strike of 1902 the operators, the financial interests, the conservative business men, were almost without exception opposed to arbitration. Many appeals to arbitrate were rejected, yet in the end both sides submitted. To what ? To the President of the United States ? No ! To public opinion, whose effective instrument the President was, and whose condemnation neither side dared to face. The President would never have ventured to take the initiative in the unprecedented, extraconstitutional course he adopted if the popular voice had not encouraged him ; nor would he have been listened to if he had.

We witnessed in England, in 1903, a most remarkable example of the development of public opinion. It was proposed to change the British tariff. Some centuries ago this would have been done by the King or his Minister ; later by Parliament. Now it was admitted on all hands that neither the King nor Parliament should have the determining voice in the decision. The House of Commons was gagged and the whole discussion was addressed to the people. Mr. Chamberlain resigned his place in the Ministry on the ground, frankly admitted, that public opinion at the time was against his policy. The Prime Minister accepted his resignation with great regret for the same reason. Then Mr. Chamberlain set himself to convert the nation, and we see at this writing going on before us, with no election pending, the unprecedented spectacle of an appeal to public opinion outside of Parliament that may alter the commercial relations of the world.

Editorial Influence Ex-President Cleveland has expressed his belief that " as a general rule the influence of newspapers in leading the judgments and determining the conduct of their readers has greatly diminished in recent years." There are more newspapers now than there were fifty years ago, and it is creditable to public opinion if it is unaffected by and even despises the teachings of many of them ; for if it responded to their appeals its impulses would often be desperately bad—and dangerous to the Republic. The influence of partisan and "organic" journalism has no doubt declined — greatly to the advantage both of the press and the country. But to say that the influence of Publicity has declined is equivalent to saying that the sun increases darkness ; that facts and truth lose their effect in proportion as they become more widely disseminated.

Editorial influence—the power of the opinions of the paper as distinguished from its news—now depends almost altogether upon public confidence in the honesty, the freedom, the fearlessness and the moral purpose of the journal itself. The people have become very discriminating in this matter. They can detect the advocate of selfish syndicates as well as the equally selfish demagogue and blatant shouter against them. They have shown their appreciation of and confidence in newspapers that are absolutely independent and inflexible in their devotion to what they believe to be right—that "expose all frauds and shams and fight all public evils and abuses " without fear and without favor.

There have been too many notable instances of the influence of newspapers in forming and leading public opinion by their editorial utterances to leave any reasonable doubt as to the continued existence of this power. And this power will persist and increase precisely in proportion to the fidelity of the newspapers to the ideal and the duty of making the press a moral force in the community, serving and battling for the people with entire sincerity, disinterestedness, freedom and fearlessness. The question whether public opinion, however formed and guided, is always to be respected and obeyed admits of but one rational answer. The theory that "the voice of the people is the voice of God " can be accepted only with important reservations. As public opinion is a variable quantity, often, as Jefferson said, "changing with the rapidity of thought," it cannot possibly always be right. Was "the voice of the people the voice of God" when it sustained human slavery in a republic dedicated to freedom? Was public opinion infallible when it sanctioned the instant enfranchisement of a race just freed from the ignorance and barbarism of slavery? Or is it right now in practically acquiescing in the disfranchisement of the same race after a generation of freedom and progress in which their right to the suffrage has been guaranteed by the Constitution? There are often errors of interpretation by those who are most anxious to go with the multitude. Mr. Bryan mistook the hysteria of the Chicago Convention for a cry of the people for cheap money.

No!—nothing is more clear than that it is often the highest duty of the press to oppose public opinion. James Bryce has truly said that " Democracies will always have demagogues ready to feed their vanity and stir passions and exaggerate the feeling of the moment. What they need is men who will swim against the stream, will tell them their faults, will urge an argument all the more forcibly because it is unwelcome."

Public opinion rightly informed is our court of last appeal. An appeal may always be safely made to it against all the public wrongs, official corruption, popular apathy or administrative faults ; and an honest press is the effective instrument in making this appeal.

Specific Instances In the days of the Tweed Ring corruption rioted in the plunder of the city treasury, and as the Ring was in possession of all the administrative machinery and the courts the people seemed helpless. But the New York *Times* exposed the evil with relentless severity and brought to bear the public opinion that routed the robbers. Tweed died in prison, and his associates sought safety in foreign countries as fugitives from justice. Another notable agitation of public opinion toward the correction of great abuses, the Lexow investigation, was due to the combined endeavors of the whole press of New York City in exposing the infamous condition of our police system.

The Beef Trust, organized to enhance the price of food and thus to enrich a great corporation by the oppression of the people, was exposed and defeated by the appeal of the New York *Herald* to the same great tribunal of public opinion. At a moment when doubt was prevalent and public opinion was peculiarly in need of enlightenment touching dangerous propositions regarding the currency, the *Evening Post* did splendid service in fighting for the maintenance of the gold standard.

Upon the publication of President Cleveland's Venezuelan message the New York *World* appealed to the good sense of the country against the war spirit which it was calculated to arouse. Opinions were invited and received by cable from the present King of England, from Mr. Gladstone, the Archbishop of Canterbury and many other dignitaries of the church and state in Great Britain, disavowing any hostile intentions toward the United States and professing the warmest sentiments of kinship and friendship. Public opinion in this country instantly responded to these fraternal expressions, and the talk of war ended in preliminaries for arbitration.

To reveal public opinion through interviews and special telegrams and promptly publish it is one of the most useful functions of the press. In 1895, deluded by the report that a certain syndicate had control of all the gold in the country, the Government was prepared to sell to that syndicate its bonds for $100,000,000 at 104½. But a telegram sent by the New York *World* to 14,000 banks brought 7,100 replies within twelve hours, and more than $235,000,000 in gold was offered to the Government in exchange for its bonds. As a result President Cleveland annulled the secret contract with the private syndicate and issued a call for popular subscriptions. The entire issue was subscribed for six times over at a price of about 112 instead of 104¼, the syndicate's offer, a gain to the Treasury of more than $7,000,000.

Agitation for a law taxing franchises was begun by *The World* newspaper in the winter of 1899. It tabulated the value of the franchises for the use of the public streets by street railways, gas companies, etc., from which the corporations reaped enormous profits and paid New York City practically nothing. Day after day the facts and figures were printed showing the magnitude of the injustice. A bill to tax the franchises as property was introduced in the State Senate. Petitions for its passage were circulated by the newspaper and received within a week 30,000 signatures. A special train was despatched from New York City to Albany, bearing delegates from organizations of workingmen and taxpayers representing 250,000 citizens and property valued at $80,000,000, to demand a report of the bill from the legislative committee in which corporation and political influence had tied it up. Many other newspapers of New York came to the support of the movement, and Governor Roosevelt, as a result of this agitation, gave his official and personal influence in its behalf through a special message to the Legislature, which secured its passage.

Here was a concrete example of a right principle, based on justice and advocated with untiring persistence. It is such agitation as this that informs, arouses and leads public opinion in achieving reforms.

The necessity and the power of persistence and reiteration in attempts to create and to render effective public opinion are not sufficiently appreciated by the press or by individual reformers. To arrest the attention, convince the judgment and enlist the sympathetic support of that great inert mass which we call the Public is a delicate and difficult task. The press, as the chief medium of Publicity, is alone equal to it. And as the press does this work intelligently, conscientiously, courageously,—disseminating intelligence as the sun diffuses light,—so shall the power of public opinion make for justice in government, for purity in politics and for a higher morality in the business and social life of the nation.

Free Lover

Sex, Marriage and Eugenics
In the Early Speeches of
Victoria Woodhull

*And the Truth will Make You Free. A Speech
on the Principles of Social Freedom*

The Scare-crows of Sexual Slavery

The Elixir of Life

*Tried as by Fire; or The True
and the False Socially*

by

Victoria Woodhull

Introduction by Michael W. Perry

Inkling Books   Seattle   2005

Contents

CHAPTER 1

"Yes, I am a Free Lover"

by Michael W. Perry

In early May of 1871, Victoria Woodhull's life seemed to be going marvelously. Under the patronage of Cornelius Vanderbilt, one of the nation's wealthiest men, her brokerage firm, Woodhull, Claflin & Company, was a financial success, providing the money for lavish parties where she met the most important people in New York City. She was also active politically. A year earlier, she began a newspaper, *Woodhull and Claflin's Weekly*, to promote herself as a candidate for President and to support voting "without distinction of sex."

Then disaster struck. On Monday, May 15 her mother Annie went to court, complaining that Woodhull's second husband, James Blood, had alienated her from her daughters and threatened, "not to go to bed until he had washed his hands in my blood." The trial was the talk of the town. In the end, there seemed to be little to the mother's charges beyond a fear she was inconvenient and might be sent to a "lunatic asylum" like Mrs. Vanderbilt.

But trials can spin out of control, particularly with a sensation-hungry press. From Blood's testimony, the public learned that Canning Woodhull, who was Woodhull's first husband, was living in the same house with her second husband, something that era found shocking and that even today might be regarded as odd. From the testimony of Tennie, Woodhull's sister, some picked up hints of sexual affairs in her claim that, "Many of the best men in [Wall] Street know my power. Commodore Vanderbilt knows my power." She meant her skill as a fortune teller, but it wasn't the wisest choice of words for an attractive woman to make, particularly since what was hinted was true. She was having an affair with the same Vanderbilt who had sent his wife to an insane asylum, so the mother's fears made sense.

The Beecher-Tilton Affair

As she often did, Woodhull decided that the best defense was to take the offensive. As Lois Underhill notes,[1] since the secrets of Woodhull's

---

1. Louis B. Underhill, *The Woman Who Ran for President: The Many Lives of Victoria Woodhull* (Binghampton: Bridge Works Pub., 1995), 179.

unconventional lifestyle would come out anyway, it was better to announce them herself and claim her behavior was based on principle. Saying nothing would lead the public to suspect she was driven by mere lust or (more likely) was using sex with powerful men to enrich herself

Woodhull made her first move in a pair of letters published in the *New York Times*. She issued a warning to the hypocrites among her critics, those who "preach against 'free love' openly, practice it secretly." In particular, she mentioned, "one man, a public teacher of eminence, who lives in concubinage with the wife of another public teacher of almost equal eminence." Some suspected the first was the popular liberal preacher of that generation, Henry Ward Beecher (1813–1887), pastor of the Plymouth Congregational Church in Brooklyn, New York. The second was thought to be Theodore Tilton (1835–1907), a member of his church and editor-in-chief of the influential *Independent*, a newspaper with as many as 500,000 readers.

In modern slang, Woodhull was 'coming out of the closet.' In her *Notorious Victoria*, Mary Gabriel notes that Woodhull had previously concealed her agreement with the radical ideas about marriage and sex being published in *Woodhull and Claflin's Weekly* by claiming she and her sister, "frequently differ widely from much which appears thus; … For ourselves we have no desire to state our convictions of truth."[2]

In the first letter, Woodhull remained vague. She limited herself to something easily defended—caring for her "sick, ailing" first husband in the home she shared with her second husband. She brought up free love only as something she advocated but not necessarily practiced, and only "in the highest and purest sense"—whatever that means. She also tried to divert attention from herself to those who secretly practiced free love while publicly denouncing it. In her second letter she also attacked differing sexual standards for men and women.

On the following three pages are Woodhull's 'coming out' letter from Saturday, May 20, 1871, reproduced exactly as it was published two days later on Monday, followed by an even angrier letter written on Tuesday, May 23 and published the following day.[3]

---

2. Mary Gabriel, *Notorious Victoria: The Life of Victoria Woodhull* (Chapel Hill: Alonquin Books, 1998), 64.
3. *New York Times*, May 22, 1871, p. 5 and May 24, 1871, p. 2.

Lady Eugenist

Feminist Eugenics
in the Speeches and Writings
of Victoria Woodhull

with

Children—Their Rights and Privileges

The Human Body (selected "Press Notices")

The Garden of Eden

Stirpiculture

Humanitarian Government

The Rapid Multiplication of the Unfit

The Scientific Propagation of the Human Race

by

Victoria Woodhull

With Introductions by Michael W. Perry

Inkling Books   Seattle   2005

Contents

Chapter 1

Was Victoria Woodhull the First Eugenist?
by Michael W. Perry

In both Europe and the United States, the nineteenth century was an exceptionally fertile time for ideas. For good and ill, all-encompassing schemes for social reorganization, such as nationalism and socialism, were nurtured until they grew strong—sadly, often strong enough to be dangerous, as the twentieth century would demonstrate.

One of those ideas was eugenics. The basic idea of eugenics, controlled breeding, has no inventor. Long before written history, people domesticated animals, selecting the most useful to parent the next generation. Cattle were chosen for meat or milk, chickens for eggs, horses for strength, and dogs for their eagerness to obey.

In historical times and particularly under the influence of Christianity, however, there was an unwillingness to extend breeding to people. For all their power, Europe's feudal lords could not mate their strongest peasant lad with their sturdiest lass, nor could they forbid the weakest from marrying and parenthood. People, however poor, still bore the image of God, and marriage was a holy sacrament. Eugenists would even complain that Medieval Catholicism had been anti-eugenic, drawing the most talented into lives of celibacy.

Other societies were different. Plato's utopia, described in his *Republic*, was to be eugenic. Nearby Sparta actually practiced a ruthless form of eugenics, killing infants who seemed unlikely to become hardy warriors. Sparta demonstrates one problem with applying ideas that work with farm animals to people. With a chicken, you know what you want—eggs. But what do you want a human to be? Isaac Newton, born tiny and premature, would have been quickly discarded in Sparta, as would Theodore Roosevelt and Winston Churchill, both sickly children who grew up to become strong and talented leaders.

But there is a sense in which eugenics has a pioneer. Pioneering an idea is like exploration and discovery. In the strictest sense, the person who discovered America was the unknown person who first crossed the land bridge from Asia. Those who want to add to "discover America" an implicit "from Europe," get caught up in debates about dates and evidences. Where did the Norse settle? Did Irish monks come here? Did Phoenicians arrive before anyone else? Columbus is unique only in that he made his exploration well known. If his three ships had been forced to return, having found no land to the west, his reputation would have been ruined. So, in that sense and even though what he found wasn't what he was looking for, Columbus discovered America. He staked his reputation on land being there and was proved right openly and publicly. That's why the world was never the same after him. It wasn't changed by Norse or Irish explorers.

That's the sense in which this book suggests Victoria Woodhull pioneered eugenics, and it's the same sense she herself claimed. She wasn't the first to come up with the idea, or the first the first to write about it. She did not get a few people to live eugenically in the small Oneida community. But she may have been the first to stake her reputation on eugenics becoming a cause. In that sense, she is the "Lady Eugenist" of this book's title, and everyone who came after, whether they admitted it or not, were her followers.

Unfortunately, that's not the official line. Almost without exception, the story of eugenics as told by historians has favored well-born, well-to-do, well-educated men, mostly English. Perhaps deceived by eugenists, who found Woodhull's prior claim embarrassing, historians have neglected the role played by women, particularly American women such as Victoria Woodhull, Charlotte Perkins Gilman, and Margaret Sanger. While I disagree strongly with virtually every premise and practice of eugenics, I believe this silence is unfair. Woodhull wanted to be credited as a eugenic pioneer—perhaps even *the* eugenic pioneer—and, as this book will demonstrate, she earned that title.

Background

First, I should explain how this book came to be. In early 2001, I was researching my second book on eugenics, *The Pivot of Civilization in Historical Perspective*[1] (from here on referred to as *Pivot*). With it, I intended to do something few had done. I wanted to take Planned Parenthood's founder, Margaret Sanger, seriously as a thinker rather than just a controversial activist. I wanted to show how what she believed fit into a fierce debate about differing birthrates in early twentieth-century America. In short, I wanted to give her a mind.

One chapter in that book[2] looked briefly (four pages) at what Victoria Woodhull had written on eugenics in an 1891 booklet, *The Rapid Multiplication of the Unfit*, republished here in its entirety (Chapter 7). At the time, that did not strike me as particularly important. The year 1891 is, after all, relatively late in the accepted history of modern eugenics. But it was while researching a different chapter that I came across something that startled me.

Chapter XII in *Pivot*, "How Bright a Torch," describes the open enthusiasm the *New York Times* once displayed for eugenics, particularly in 1912 when its coverage of the topic peaked, perhaps because of a prestigious eugenics conference held in London that summer. Given the newspaper's enthusiasm for getting rid of those it regarded as unfit, I decided to see how it covered *Buck*

---

1. Michael W. Perry, ed. *The Pivot of Civilization in Historical Perspective* (Seattle: Inkling Books, 2001). Page references to *Pivot* are to the wide-format paperback rather than the hardback.
2. *Pivot*, Chapter IV, "The Rapid Multiplication of the Unfit."

v. Bell, the infamous 1927 U.S. Supreme Court decision that declared eugenic sterilization constitutional. Had its zeal waned in the intervening fifteen years?

It had not. Speaking as if it defined all that was true and proper, the newspaper could not have been more approving. Two of the headlines were "Right to Protect Society" and "Justice Holmes Draws Analogy to Compulsory Vaccination in Woman's Case." The *Times* clearly agreed with the author of the opinion. Had it thought otherwise, it could have pointed out a critical difference between a Massachusetts vaccination law cited in the opinion and Virginia's sterilization law. Anyone opposed to being vaccinated could pay a five dollar fine and be left alone. The sterilization law offered no such escape. And so no one would think that forced eugenic sterilization was in the least controversial, the *Times* buried the story deep inside the paper near an article about another court's decision to ban the use of "chain coupons" in "silk stockings sales."[3]

The paper's coverage did not end there. Five days later, the *Times* ran an article by an Associated Press reporter in Brighton, England who, gushing with praise, had interviewed Victorian Woodhull, now bearing the name Martin. What drew my attention were the following remarks. (Bolding added.)

… Time has not dimmed the eyes of this spirited woman who, with her sister, the late Lady Cook, formerly Tennessee Claflin, was the first woman broker in New York and lectured and published *Claflin's Weekly* **in support of equal suffrage and eugenics before they both came to England.**…

Mrs. Martin, who **wrote and lectured for thirty years on eugenics,** remarked that she was pleased to read that the Virginia Eugenics law had succeeded in establishing the right to sterilize the feeble-minded.

"**I advocated that fifty years ago** in my book, *Marriage of the Unfit*," she said. "I am also glad that parents are now beginning to instruct their adolescent children in the facts of life. My sister, Tennessee, and I were mercilessly slandered fifty years ago, when **we dared to advocate women's emancipation and discussed eugenics** in America, but time has proved that we were right."[4]

I was surprised by two things Woodhull said. The first was her claim to have been promoting eugenics some "fifty years ago" (1877), which she said was before it "came to England." That suggested she promoted it in the U.S. through her public lectures and in *Woodhull and Claflin's Weekly* (1870–76), and that she had brought those ideas with her when she moved to England in 1877.

I wondered at the time if she was being honest or just playing her usual "I was the first woman to…" game. I have since discovered she was right. A speech

---

3 . "Upholds Operating on Feeble-Minded." *New York Times* (May 3, 1927), 19. In *Pivot*, 31.
4 . "Says Voting at 25 is 'Young Enough.'" *New York Times* (May 3, 1927), pt. 2, p. 6. In *Pivot*, 31. For a facsimile, see page 56 in this book. I could not find *Marriage of the Unfit*. She may have meant *The Rapid Multiplication of the Unfit*, or it may have been a pamphlet printed in the 1870s in such small quantities that no copy survives today.

she made in 1871, republished in Chapter 2 of this book, is clearly eugenic. Newspapers from the 1870s, quoted in Chapter 3, mention eugenic ideas in speeches she gave across the U.S. Finally, as you can see from the title page of last booklet in this collection (Chapter 8), as least as early 1893 she claimed to have lectured on eugenics "throughout America, from 1870 to 1876."

The second odd remark was that Woodhull and her sister "dared to advocate women's emancipation and discussed eugenics." How could she link emancipation with eugenics? For eugenics to succeed, ten to twenty percent of women must be kept from having any children, and perhaps another twenty to thirty percent must be kept from having more than two. That's regimentation rather than emancipation. Later we'll see what she meant.

The Role of Francis Galton

Although Francis Galton (1822–1911) would not coin the term "eugenics" until 1883, historians tell us that eugenics began in England with Galton's 1865 article in *Macmillan's Magazine* entitled "Hereditary Talent and Character," That's why I included extracts from it as the first appendix in my edition of G. K. Chesterton's 1922 *Eugenics and Other Evils*.[5]

Woodhull's own remarks, however, suggest the history of eugenics may be more complicated. Was Galton's early article that significant, or was there an independent history of eugenics in the United States, one that helped start the movement in England, and one whose chief spokesman was a woman from a far less prestigious background than Galton? After all, the idea of breeding people like farmers mate their livestock isn't hard to imagine, however distasteful many of us now find it. It needs neither Darwin nor Galton for inspiration.

From Galton's day until the present, eugenists certainly have not been happy about suggestions that they might be linked to Woodhull, a controversial speaker-for-hire. In a 1976 book supported by the Council of the Eugenics Society, G. R. Searle dismisses Woodhull as little more than an "engaging charlatan." "Stirpiculture" (Chapter 5) and "scientific propagation" (Chapter 8) were two early terms for what later came to be called "eugenics." (Bolding added.)

Another embarrassment to sober men like Galton was the American, Victoria Woodhull-Martin, an engaging charlatan, whose bizarre career took her through three marriages, numerous liaisons, several well-publicized scandals, an attempt to stand as President of the United States, and advocacy of spiritualism, elixirs of life, communism, sex equality, free love—**and stirpiculture.** But, despite her invocations of "science," Mrs. Woodhull-Martin had no authority to pontificate on matters of human inheritance, and many of her observations on this subject were ill-formed and nonsensical. **It was the backing of responsible and established scientific men which was essential to the progress of eugenics.** All this had to wait until

5. G. K. Chesterton, *Eugenics and Other Evils* (Seattle: Inkling Books, 2000), 123–26.

such a time as biologists had acquired an understanding of heredity that would enable them to explain how parents transmitted certain of the physical and intellectual qualities to their offspring. Not until the Edwardian period had the scientific groundwork been sufficiently well laid for eugenics to become a plausible political creed.[6]

"Established scientific men"—that's like saying that discoveries of new lands can only be done by those who belong to the Royal Geographic Society. Uncredentialed men and particularly women do not count, no matter how early they visit or how widely they describe their travels when they return. Yes, some of Woodhull's ideas were "bizarre," and I don't hesitate to point that out. But Columbus' geography was so bizarre, he thought he had reached the East Indies, even though an entire continent and an ocean stood in his way. And most of Woodhull's eugenic ideas weren't that out of line with what the scientists and medical men of her day believed. Some stand up to scrutiny at least as well as those championed by the more scientifically credentialed eugenists. Here's what Searle sniffed about Woodhull in an endnote.

> Many of her 'scientific' theories, in fact, ran counter to the central propositions of the eugenists, e.g. 'The most active agent in generating the unfit is fatigue poison…'; much 'family generation… is due to physical exhaustion from overwork or the lack of sufficient light and fresh air;' see V. C. Woodhull-Martin, *The Rapid Multiplication of the Unfit* (1891), p. 10. It is Mrs. Woodhull-Martin's oft-repeated contention that those who were unfit through fatigue produced degenerate offspring. Although she lived the latter part of her life in London, where she edited a weekly, *The Humanitarian*, H. G. Wells is the only British writer known to me to acknowledge any debt to her; see his *Mankind in the Making* (1903), p. 39.

Notice that Serle's main objection to Woodhull was that what she said "ran counter to the central propositions of the eugenists" that hereditary was everything and environment counted for little. Unlike Woodhull, who seemed to grab ideas from everywhere with little concern for their source, many eugenists were a prissy lot, liking their theories wrapped up in neat packages. But few in medicine today would fault her for attacking "fatigue poison." Exhaustion is an indication that a child's parents aren't getting nutritious food, enough rest, or "sufficient light and fresh air," for their unborn child's health. An unborn baby may not be influenced by a mother in all the ways Woodhull assumed. But she was right in her claim that the influence wasn't simply genetic.

Given the importance of H. G. Well's own popularization of eugenics from 1901 on, if Woodhull had only influenced him, she would have accomplished

---

6. G. R. Searle, *Eugenics and Politics in Britain 1900–1914* (Leyden: Noordhoff International Publishing, 1976), 5–6. The Edwardian period ran from 1901–10, with some extending it to World War I. Notice those "responsible and established scientific men" were waiting for evidence to render "plausible" a "political creed" they already believed—in the case of Galton since 1865. That's more ideological than scientific.

quite a bit. The year before *Mankind in the Making* (1903) was published as a book, it was serialized in *Cosmopolitan* magazine, reaching the American equivalent of what Wells called "titled ladies of liberal outlook." (Those women later provided support for Margaret Sanger's birth control movement.) But Wells credited Woodhull with more than that. He contrasted Francis Galton's 1901 Huxley Lecture to the Anthropological Institute, which was heard by a few, with Woodhull's earlier lectures and writings before a much wider audience. Of course, he also noted that the queer "absurdity and pretentiousness" of many the writers she found for her cause made him wish it would be taken up by "sober and honest men"—a term that in Wellesian meant ruthless and unprincipled men who knew how to brush aside opposition and get things done.

> At a more popular level Mrs. Victoria Woodhull Martin has battled bravely in the cause of the same foregone conclusion. The work of telling the world what it knows to be true will never want self-sacrificing workers. *The Humanitarian* was her monthly organ of propaganda. Within its cover, which presented a luminiferous stark ideal of exemplary muscularity, popular preachers, popular bishops, and popular anthropologists vied with titled ladies of liberal outlook in the service of this conception. There was much therein about the Rapid Multiplication of the Unfit, a phrase never properly explained, and I must confess that the transitory presence of this instructive little magazine in my house, month after month (it is now, unhappily, dead), did much to direct my attention to the gaps and difficulties that intervene between the general proposition and its practical application by sober and honest men. One took it up and asked time after time, "Why should there be this queer flavour of absurdity and pretentiousness about the thing?" Before the *Humanitarian* period I was entirely in agreement with the *Humanitarian*'s cause. It seemed to me then that to prevent the multiplication of people below a certain standard, and to encourage the multiplication of exceptionally superior people, was the only real and permanent way of mending the ills of the world. I think that still. In that way man has risen from the beasts, and in that way men will rise to be over-men. In those days I asked in amazement why this thing was not done, and talked the usual nonsense about the obduracy and stupidity of the world. It is only after a considerable amount of thought and inquiry that I am beginning to understand why for many generations, perhaps, nothing of the sort can possibly be done except in the most marginal and tentative manner.[7]

Wells was a eugenic moderate, skeptical that, given our current state of knowledge and our existing political institutions, much could be done to improve the world "except in the most marginal and tentative manner." He would express similar doubts in the introduction he wrote for Margaret Sanger's 1922 *The Pivot of Civilization*. Wells rested his hope in a world run by a technocratic elite that would adopt a clever but covert eugenic scheme. From 1901 on, in

---

7. H. G. Wells, *Mankind in the Making* (New York: C. Scribner's Sons, 1904), 36–7.

The Pivot of Civilization
In Historical Perspective

The Birth Control Classic

by
Margaret Sanger

Edited by
Michael W. Perry

With Articles by Others Including:

Victoria Woodhull Martin, H. G. Wells, G. B. Shaw, Theodore Roosevelt, Ellen Key, Henry Goddard, G. K. Chesterton, Charlotte Perkins Gilman, Archbishop Patrick Hayes, and Oliver Wendell Holmes, Jr.

Inkling Books   Seattle   2003

Contents

Historical Perspective

The Pivot of Civilization

by Margaret Sanger

Preface

Time magazine's remarkable account of Margaret Sanger's life, published the week after her death on September 6, 1966, illustrates why this book was written.

> Family planning by contraception was the cause, Margaret Sanger was its champion. Half a century ago, when she raised the banners of her lonely crusade, she was lacerated from the pulpits as a "lascivious monster" bent on "murdering" unborn children. Birth control, a phrase she herself invented, was unmentionable, immoral and illegal. It was a federal crime merely to send information about it through the mails. She was arrested eight times. Her zeal led to the breakup of her first marriage. Yet when she died last week of arteriosclerosis in Tucson at the age of 82, her vision had been realized beyond her dreams. Birth control, which to her meant the right of every woman to control the size of her own family, had become accepted in the U.S. and was spreading rapidly throughout the world.[1]

What is remarkable is that virtually everything this respected news magazine said about her life was not only false, it was easily demonstrated to be so.

Some mistakes are minor. Sanger didn't coin the term "birth control," much less get everyone to talking about a topic previously "unmentionable." She merely publicized the term as an easy way to refer to a something that had been an obsession of the nation's 'chattering classes' for over a decade. In fact, the first 17 chapters in this book quote extensively from magazine articles and books that predate Sanger's active public life and each touches, directly or indirectly, on the subject. In addition, Sanger's crusade was not only far from lonely, it soon elevated her into the ranks of that 'enlightened and thoughtful' class of people who consider their opinions superior to those of the general run of humanity.

Other mistakes are more serious. Her marriage was not destroyed by her "zeal" for the cause. Her first husband did jail time for promoting birth control before she did. Like most spouses, he simply couldn't cope with her rampant sexual promiscuity. That matters, because in that era a critical part of the debate over birth control centered on whether it would encourage promiscuity. Catholics claimed it would. Liberals—though they may have known otherwise—denied any such link. Sanger's own behavior hints at what we now know is true, that the Catholics and their religious allies were right. In fact, the organization that Sanger founded, Planned Parenthood, now gets public money to counter with chemistry a teen lifestyle it helps to promote. That's a bit like a tobacco company getting a federal subsidy to treat lung cancer.

Then there is the much more serious matter of abortion. Alas, in its endless pursuit of fashion, upper-Manhattan style, *Time* misplaced a pair of quotation marks. They were put around "murdering" rather than "unborn children." The pretense that what lives in the womb was of an uncertain nature was not yet dogma. Sanger's conservative religious critics got it wrong, *Time* told us, when they claimed that Sanger wanted abortion legalized. Birth control, everyone who was anyone then knew, was intended to prevent what many 1960s liberals were still calling the "evil of abortion." As propaganda, it was clever. At the time of Sanger's death, federally funded family planning was promoted as a counter to abortion rather than its prelude.

It is true that you can find quite a bit of material to back up *Time*'s claims in the pages of Sanger's own magazine, *Birth Control Review*. In the March, 1925 issue, for instance, a physician and board member in the American Birth Control League said: "Not only has Birth Control nothing in common with Abortion, but it is a weapon of the greatest value in fighting this evil."[2] The following year the magazine would explain: "Birth control is not abortion. Abortion is the taking of life after conception; Birth Control is the prevention of conception."[3]

---

1. "Every Child a Wanted Child," *Time* (Sept. 16, 1966), 96.

2. Benjamin T. Tilton, "Birth Control as a Prevention of Abortion," *Birth Control Review* (Mar. 1925), 71.

Earlier Sanger did call for abortion. In 1915, Marie Stopes, Sanger's British counterpart, wrote to her while gathering signatures of prominent people to induce President Wilson to intervene in Sanger's prosecution for sending her fierce 1914 magazine, *Woman Rebel* through the mail. "I am getting on with my letter to your President," she wrote, "but it is slower and more difficult than I expect[ed] chiefly because of what you said about abortion. If *only* you had left that out!"[4] Sanger did not need anyone to teach her how to lie, but she did need to know when to lie. Had the time for its legalization come a bit sooner, her zeal to get rid of undesirables would have been more than enough to cross the conception gap.

Those who read Sanger carefully can sense that she saw abortion complications and deaths as little more than a tool to batter her "puritanical" and "masculine-minded"[5] opponents. In a 1946 letter, she described that technique when she explained how she handled Catholics: refusing to be on the same platform with them, "saying they were vulgar," and her primary technique— "Attack. Accuse them of all the evils on earth, including abortions and war."[6] Her oft-repeated claim that birth control would do away with abortion was nonsense. Even today's much better technologies haven't done that.

In the late 1930s, this deception may have become more difficult to maintain. It was true that in a February 1938 speech in Tucson, Sanger did claim that the birth control movement, "has advocated definite means to eradicate abortion,"[7] and in May of the next year she'd write "Destroy" on a letter from someone with the Abortion Law Reform Association in London.[8] But in the fall of 1939, a colleague named Clarence Gamble was in contact with her about an African folk remedy that he claimed had produced abortions "in 13 out of the 15" pregnancies.[9]

In his grim tale of totalitarian rule, *1984,* George Orwell would blast the British left ("INGSOC" in the novel is English socialism) for the speed with which it could not only shift its opinion, but deny that it had ever believed what it had recently been saying. *Time*'s shifting stance on Sanger and abortion illustrates just that sort of behavior. Much as a totalitarian state has a Big Brother who can do no wrong, progressive thought has 'brave pioneers' like Sanger who serve humanity by defying convention. That is the 'story' that journalists and biographers are expected to write, often in defiance of the facts.

For virtually all Sanger's adult life, the politically correct story was that abortion was an 'evil' created by 'reactionaries' opposing the spread of birth control. At a superficial level that seemed true. A survey of writings on birth control and similar topics from late nineteen century to about 1960 might find feminists and their allies often expressing a deep concern for the fate of children as yet unborn.[10] Only the more astute would notice that the "potential child" they championed was merely a symbol for the improved humanity they intended to breed. In the end, they could not maintain a pretense so out of line with their beliefs. Abortion fit all too well with the 'might makes right' mindset of evolution, just as the belief that a person is a person no matter how small, weak, or unwanted fits with Judeo-Christian beliefs.

But this book is not about legalized abortion. Except for a few radical feminists, particularly in Germany, it wasn't a major issue during the period covered by this book—from the 1870s until the early 1930s—so it won't be a major issue in this book. Honestly or dishonestly, virtually all those involved in the debates we will cover professed a horror of abortion. Even, Charlotte Perkins Gilman, perhaps the premier feminist intellectual of the early twentieth century, portrayed it as something so terrible it could exist only because men forced it on women.

The central focus of this book is on something quite different. We will be looking at the motivations that drove Sanger, the birth control movement, and its many allies. This is where the story gets *very* interesting. While progressive movements can be ruthless at covering up evils they did in the past, they are often quite candid (at least among themselves) about the currently fashionable causes they champion—even causes that later come to be

---

3. "Birth Control Primer," *Birth Control Review* (Jan. 1926), n.p.

4. Marie Stopes to Margaret Sanger, Sept. 15, 1914, Sanger/Smith microfilm, S01:0459.

5. For example: Margaret Sanger, "Birth Control or Abortion?" *Birth Control Review* (Dec. 1918), 3.

6. Margaret Sanger to Anna Jane Phillips Shuman, 1946. Sanger/Smith microfilm, C08:0143.

7. Margaret Sanger, speech to the Mother's Health Center, Tucson, Arizona, Feb. 8, 1938, Sanger/Smith microfilm, S71:0975.

8. Janet Chance to Margaret Sanger, May 12, 1939, Sanger/Smith microfilm, S16:0805.

9. Clarence Gamble to Margaret Sanger, Oct. 31, 1939. Sanger/Smith microfilm, C06:1068. The correspondence went on for about a year, but Sanger seemed more interested in a Hungarian spermatoxin that had been tested on "about a hundred women and numerous rabbits." She hoped that idea could get further testing using money intended for "the colored problem in the South." Sanger to Gamble, Nov. 5, 1939, Sanger/Smith microfilm, C06:1069. Though the letter has no obvious racist 'smoking gun,' the fact that she was discussing Southern blacks probably explains why it was headed, "Confidential for C.J.G."

10. For an example, see Chapter X, "The Century of the Child," by Ellen Key, a Swedish feminist.

regarded as great evils. As we will see, eugenics, a kissing cousin of birth control, is a good example.

One reason is arrogance. Believing themselves right, they lack the restraint that most people display. They fail to ask themselves, "But is what I believe so certain that I must force my agenda on others?" In this book you will find writer after writer discussing not whether he and his sort has the right to decide who has children—that is assumed as a matter of course—but what criteria and techniques ought to be used by a few intent on making that decision for the many. Eugenists advocated one set of criteria, liberals and socialists slightly different rationale, and feminists such as Sanger yet another. Each had its own axe to grind, but that axe is inevitably being sharpened to be used on the reproductive powers of others. Their minds, it seems, could follow no other paths.

In recent years, the growing weight that all-too-obvious fact has made it increasingly difficult in the academic world to portray Sanger as a champion of women's rights. Where biographers and historians go from there often depends on their political beliefs. Those on the left blame Sanger's contacts with large capitalists such as the Rockefellers, neglecting to mention that all her life Sanger drew warm support from socialists and liberals. Others claim, rather belatedly, that a woman who was long championed as a feminist was never really one. Again they get it wrong. Sanger made an excellent case for why career-oriented feminists should support restrictions on other women's childbearing that remains as persuasive today as it was in the 1920s.

The result is a muddle, with various groups from that period being confused with one another. Race suiciders, eugenists, Social Darwinians, and birth controllers are jumbled together with the beliefs of one attributed to another. Some of the worst offenders remain uncriticized, while the more benign are targeted as bigots.

In their histories of birth control, two deservedly well-respected scholars make the first mistake, misattributing the same quote to Sanger. Both claim that in the May 1919 issue of *Birth Control Review* Sanger wrote, "More children from the fit, less from the unfit—that is the chief issue in Birth Control."[11] Anyone who knew Sanger would know that the first clause would *never* pass her lips. Her life was dedicated to preventing just that sort of "cradle race." Make sure the unfit have fewer children— "Yes!"—she would say. But there must be no pressure on

her class to have more children. The quote they both misattribute was taken from an *American Medicine* editorial that Sanger reprinted and represents what eugenists were saying. Though Sanger disagreed vehemently with the "positive" measures eugenists advocated, they were allies and had to be humored. In the long run, she knew she had little to fear from eugenists. Their zeal for pressuring the 'better' sort of people to have more children was so anemic that many of them had few or no children.

The final position for those wanting to whitewash Sanger is less than impressive. In Sanger's day, we are told, almost everyone was a bigot and a racist. Sanger, for all the goodness of her heart, was caught up in her culture and could not escape. Under such reasoning, Sanger, once considered a radical of radicals, wasn't radical enough. Again, the truth lies elsewhere. The great bulk of Americans never adopted the nasty attitudes that drove Sanger and her supporters. While certainly not perfect, they simply weren't that prejudiced.

An excellent example is an oft-reprinted 1904 book entitled *The Laws of Sex Life and Heredity or Eugenics*. Not only was this Ohio-published book more candid about many sexual matters than Sanger typically was (demolishing the illusion that the era was sexually repressed), but the eugenics it advocated was far milder and vastly more tolerant than what you will read in this book. True, the publisher did seem to have been reading the nation's elite press. The opening briefly warns of the dangers of "feeble-mindedness." But none of that reappears in the text. (Feeble-minded is not even listed in the index.) Instead, the book presents a point of view congenial to religious conservatives, including the Women's Christian Temperance Union, which endorsed it. Readers are assured that the "law of inheritance" is "not an invariable one," and "its force must not be overestimated."[12] Health problems are not only regarded as predominately environmental, they are treated as something the average person can handle. There is no call for scientific dictates or new religions of the sort that appealed to Sanger and her colleagues.

So keep in mind as you read this book that the attitudes you see displayed here were held only by an affluent, educated, and well-connected few who were obsessed with improving the world by manipulating the birthrates of others. Obvious as that may seem to those who read the articles collected here, the average Ameri-

11. The references are David Kennedy, *Birth Control in America,* 115; and Linda Gordon, *Woman's Body, Woman's Right,* 281. Both books are well worth reading. The article Sanger did publish in *American Medicine* was reprinted two pages earlier.

12. T. W. Shannon, *The Laws of Sex Life and Heredity or Eugenics.*(Marietta, Ohio: S. A. Mullikin, 1917), 3, 235. The book's old fashioned frankness about sex led Doubleday to republish it in 1970.

cans of that day did not grasp what Sanger's real agenda was. Her claims about giving poor mothers 'choice' was enough to cloud their far more tolerant minds. Because they did not think someone else's family size was any of their business, they had trouble believing anyone else would be obsessed with such things. They were wrong, tragically wrong.

History is clear about one thing. In the era covered by this book, open cultural and genetic intolerance was far more common among the progressive-minded than among the religious conservatives who were Sanger's most vocal opponents.[13]

You get taste of that in an article in the *New York Times* on the last Thursday of February, 1924. A Rev. Charles Francis Potter of the West Side Unitarian Church, the paper said, was announcing his plan for "a new, all-American Bible." In a chilling prelude to what would soon be happening in Germany, this liberal clergyman made it clear that there would be no place within its pages for foreigners, and particularly not for "the literature of a Semitic nation of 2,000 years ago." He went on to add: "If we are to have the Bible taught in our American schools, let it be the American Bible." Did the *Times* go to a liberal to counter this nasty bit of anti-Semitism? No, they went to Dr. John Straton, the city's best known fundamentalist preacher.[14] As we will see, many on the political left felt threatened by waves of immigrants bringing in their tradition-minded culture and more than a few of those immigrants were religious Jews.

The *Times* choice of a religious conservative to defend other cultures and races wasn't a fluke. In July of the following year, *Forum* magazine published an article by the famous fundamentalist politician, William Jennings Bryan, entitled "Mr. Bryan Speaks to Darwin." In the

same issue, their "Toasts" section described a lecture by the Rev. William R. Inge, a friend of Sanger and the Anglican church hierarchy's boldest birth control supporter. As it described what the Rev. Inge had said, the magazine noted, "it would be difficult to find in all Christendom a greater contrast between the beliefs of two men both professing the same faith" than Bryan and Inge.[15]

They zeroed in on the critical difference. At that time Bryan was evolution's best known foe. In contrast, Inge was "a confirmed evolutionist" and "a believer in the possibility of improving the human race through eugenics." The political labels given the two men reflect this difference. Bryan's championing of ordinary people earned him the title, "The Great Commoner." In contrast, Igne's elitist whining about social ills gave the well-known Dean of St. Paul's Cathedral in London the nickname the "Gloomy Dean."

In his lecture, Inge championed themes we will encounter repeatedly in this book. There was, for instance, the issue of 'old stock' Americans being overwhelmed by waves of inferior immigrants: "America, I am afraid, is becoming less Anglo-Saxon every year. . . . I know the new immigration laws are designed to protect the old tradition, and I hope they will preserve the dominance of the northern European stock. I don't mean just the English—many Englishmen are not particularly desirable—but the Scandinavians, the Dutch, and the better sort of Germans, also."

At that point, this champion of northern European supremacy was challenged by a representative from another group that opposed birth controllers, Rev. Cornelius C. Clifford, pastor of a Roman Catholic church in New Jersey. "I am puzzled to know," Clifford asked, "upon what biological ground your assumption of a superior northern type rests, and, if you will pardon me, I do not believe it has a leg to stand on." Refusing to back down, Inge replied that, "I doubt whether southern Mediterraneans are desirable people to introduce into this country." Or be permitted to have large families once they arrive, we might add. It's easy to see why Inge and Sanger got along so fabulously.

Forum got it exactly right. The difference between Bryan and Inge hinged on their views about evolution. The "biological ground" of Inge's assumption was evolution. It is true that Darwin's basic theory did not in itself prove that Northern Europeans were superior to Southern or Eastern Europeans. But it did claim as scientific truth that some human groups were 'fit' and others 'unfit.'

---

13. It is easy to suspect that the same pattern continues today despite rhetoric about "diversity" and "pluralism." Why are some obsessed with a topic that most Americans find boring? And why isn't pluralism given its correct meaning—one in which laws concerning family, marriage and education are decided by ethnic and religious groups rather than dictated by the state?

14. "Plans New Bible for America," *New York Times* (Feb. 28, 1924), 21. The day before, the *Times* gave Potter's Jew-free 'new bible' front-page coverage. Like Inge, described next, Potter had ties to Sanger. In November of that year, she would invite him to speak at a meeting she was holding. (Sanger to Francis Potter, Nov. 11, 1924, Sanger/Smith microfilm, C03:0225.) Rev. Potter also attended the Scopes Monkey trial and promoted himself as an expert on evolution and religion. For pointing me to the 'new bible' controversy, I am indebted to Carlton J. H. Hayes, *Essays on Nationalism* (New York: Macmillan, 1926), 121–122.

---

15. "Toasts," *Forum* 74 (July 1925), n. p. Inge described himself as a Liberal.

Instinctively, evolution's true believers sought to discover the 'holy grail' of their secular religion—which is which? Once on that path, what grouping is more biologically apt than race or, within races, economic classes? From belief in evolution to zeal for eugenics, sterilization or birth control was but a small step.

In contrast, for those whose worldview was essentially biblical—the old Jewish one—all the measures of fitness that so impressed their foes, a comfortable financial state, alleged intelligence, artistic genius and the like, were simply not that important. In Chapter XXI, we will see a quote that sums up the contrast: "Heredity! Heredity! The word has rung in my ears until I am sick of it. There is just one heredity in this world of ours—we are the children of God." Harvard's Edward East might sneeringly dismiss that as no more than a "burst of emotion," but its implications, if rejected, are enormous.

Deprived of a theological reason for attaching genuine value *all* to human lives, the alternatives are bleak. We can claim, with the crudest of Social Darwinians, that rights belong only to those who can defend them—as Justice Holmes does in Chapter XXIII. Or we can develop a criteria that gives an illusion of value: intelligence, foresight, efficiency or whatever. This book is filled with the champions of that point of view. All share the same flaw—the criteria is relative. Whether it is silly, like Nazism's fascination with blue-eyed blonds, or more complex, involving intelligence tests and measures of professional success, the criteria always measures some against others. "Intelligent" always means "more intelligent than." As Inge's remarks indicate, that thinking can take a nasty turn, particularly when attention turns to immigration or differing birthrates. Modern evolution has replaced its original belief in the importance of mere survival with a more nuanced one involving the number of surviving offspring. He who dies with the most living offspring wins the new evolutionary game. The result is a nasty urge to squelch the birthrate of others.

A disclaimer needs to be added. The danger does *not* lie in a vague assent to evolutionary theory. Much more is required. Several of those in this book got it right when they wrote of founding a new religion. It is only when belief in evolution becomes the central, defining dogma of one's life that serious problems develop.

The resulting thought process isn't hard to follow. Evolution splits each species into fit and unfit. Who belongs to each? As we will see, therein lies much nastiness. Next comes evolution's attempt to put an optimistic spin on a nature that seems "red with tooth and claw." To do that, the death of the unfit is linked to progress—the

ones who die *ought* to die. Any glorification of death has chilling implications, especially when a mindset develops that this progress-inducing natural culling is no longer taking place. What if virtually every child born now grows to reproductive adulthood? Evolution, it seems, has come to an end. Does that mean biological progress has stopped? Certainly. Is evolutionary disaster upon us? Quite possibly. What can be done to prevent this disaster? That's what most of those in this book discuss. You find the roots of this reasoning in the very last words of Charles Darwin's *The Origin of Species*.

> Thus, from the war of nature, from famine and death, the most exalted object of which we are capable of conceiving, namely, the production of the higher animals, directly follows. There is a grandeur in this view of life, with its several powers, having been originally breathed by the Creator into a few forms or into one; and that, whilst this planet has gone cycling on according to the fixed law of gravity, from so simple a beginning endless forms most beautiful and most wonderful have been, and are being evolved.

Note how Darwin praised his new theory, referring to its "grandeur" and to the "most beautiful and most wonderful" results it created. Good, he was saying, could come out of the twin evils of "famine and death."

But is that really true? Exactly who benefits by evolution? Does the slow-footed little bunny who is devoured by a better evolved wolf? Obviously not. But, you say, how about the speedier bunny who does evade the wolf, at least until he grows old? Again the answer is a clear no. The same process that evolves the bunny also evolves the wolf. The result is a biological 'arms race' with no real winners. The deadly race between predator and prey merely moves a faster pace.

Viewed from the perspective of individuals within a species, evolution seems to have only victims. Who are the winners? Darwin and his kin certainly are. As the tellers of this grand story, they win our adoration. That was and remains one of evolution's chief attractions within the scientific community—one that blinds them to just how gruesome their tale really is.

Another winner are those who, like Darwin, see themselves at the apex not just of the "higher animals" but of humanity itself. But, as we have noted, that is where the nastiness begins. Follow Darwin and you can find beauty in the survival of the fittest only by growing indifferent (or worse) to the deaths of the unfit. In the end what is idealized and even worshiped is an abstraction, an ever-evolving, ever-improving, almost god-like humanity. To that abstraction living, breathing people must be sacrificed. Some see beauty in that. Others find it monstrous.

At this point a few cautions are needed. Yes, many of the ideas advanced in this book do sound silly today. Virtually no American alive claims, with Rev. Inge, that southern Italians make bad citizens (though we do still hear the closely linked idea that Catholicism is dangerous). Nor do we hear much about the threat of rapidly multiplying feeble-minded people. Though some still think that way, population control replaced eugenics as the public rationale in the 1950s and 1960s and that, in turn was replaced by arguments centered on the self-fulfillment and 'choice' in the 1970s.

The shift is easy to track. In 1962, Alan Guttmacher, former vice-president of the American Eugenics Association, assumed the presidency of Planned Parenthood. Soon, a 'population bomb' hysteria (and later rhetoric about environmental doom) was driving public policy. In 1969, a medical news magazine revealed what was really going on when it quoted Guttmacher warning that if "voluntary means" did not achieve the desired goals, "Each country will have to decide its own form of coercion and determine when and how it should be employed. At present, the means available are compulsory sterilization and compulsory abortion. Perhaps some day a way of enforcing compulsory birth control will be feasible."[16] Think of women being dragged into a medical clinic and forcibly sterilized or aborted and you capture his intent. Beneath the rhetoric about "choice" their real agenda was just that ugly.

"But," you may say, "Planned Parenthood is about giving women reproductive choices. How can the second most important individual in the organization's history talk about compulsion. The evening news, my local paper, and anyone who is anyone tells me that. You could get a hundred Noble Prize winners to sign a paper stating just that. After all they call themselves 'prochoice' don't they."

Yes, 'prochoice' singular, not 'prochoices' plural. The distinction is *extremely* important. Coercion, one step short of compulsion, means that you narrow someone's choices, so those targeted feel that they have only one option—not having a child. That's what Sanger intended to do with birth control, as we will see repeatedly in the portions of this book that she wrote, so why should it be surprising that Guttmacher felt the same? And, whether

you have heard it or not, Sanger's bigotry is old news. Academically, the issue was settled very quietly during the 1970s. And in that silence lies truth. If Sanger was so anti-choice, why hasn't she been properly demonized by the "prochoice" movement? And why haven't they praised the "religious right" for the role it played in blocking what Sanger intended to do to our parents and grandparents?

Instead, the sorts of people who once championed Sanger's cause now focus on damage control. Any awareness of Sanger's real agenda must be confined to as small a circle as possible. As dramatic as the events in this book are, don't expect them to become the theme of a hard-hitting network TV documentary. Even more important, the general population must kept from realizing that from certain perspectives—feminist, liberal and socialist—what Sanger was doing is not only reasonable but absolutely necessary. That is precisely why those groups supported her so enthusiastically. Doubt that? Then read on. In this book we will let them explain, in their own words, why they intended to control—with whatever level of coercion was necessary—just who has children. In fact, most of the text of this book is theirs. To ensure that what they say is not ripped out of context, they are allowed to go on for page after page explaining what they believe in great detail. As unpleasant as it is, they have as much right to be understood as you and I have a right to understand them and what they intended to do.

Finally, some may find this book confusing. Expecting an author or editor to shape everything to one point of view, they will find the presence of many well-argued but widely differing views upsetting. They want a Sanger who was either a saint or a devil. I give them Sanger as she actually was and properly situated in the controversies of her day. View the world through a Malthusian and Darwinian lens, and Sanger was a saint, struggling to prevent evolutionary and social disaster. View her through the lens of her religious foes, and she was a devil trying to dictate, though coercion and deception, who could become a parent. It is that simple. But no one should insult her intelligence by claiming the outlandish things that many of her more adoring biographers have said, or that *Time* magazine printed in her obituary. Whether we agreed or disagree with what she was trying to do, she needs to be treated with respect and honesty.

With that I leave you with this book in the hope you will find it as stimulating to read as it has been for me to write and edit.

—Michael W. Perry, Seattle, August 28, 2003

---

16. "Outlook," *Medical World News* (June 6, 1969), 11. "Voluntary means" could include manipulating circumstances to pressure undesired groups into having fewer children. Compulsory means are those that can be imposed efficiently on the unwilling. The arrival of long-term injectable contraceptives such as Depro Provera closed the only gap in the technological arsenal.

HISTORICAL PERSPECTIVE

XXVI

An Answer to Mr. Roosevelt

1917

Margaret Sanger

President, American Birth Control League

The best thing that the modern American college does for young men or young women is to make of them highly sensitized individuals, keenly aware of their responsibility to society. They quickly perceive that they have other duties toward the State than procreation of the kind blindly practised by the immigrant from Europe. They cannot be deluded into thinking quantity superior to quality.

An Answer to Mr. Roosevelt—1917

Margaret Sanger, "An Answer to Mr. Roosevelt." *Birth Control Review* (Dec. 1917), 13–14. The "Ed." in the next paragraph is an editor at *Birth Control Review.*

(In the October issue of the *Metropolitan Magazine* appeared an article by former-President Roosevelt, entitled "Birth Control—From the Positive Side." It revealed a desire to arrive at the same results of race betterment which we advocate. It swept aside, however, not only the principle of voluntary motherhood, but the existing racial and class conditions[1] which must be taken into consideration if the desired end is to be attained. The following is Margaret Sanger's reply, which appears in the December number of the *Metropolitan.*—Ed.)

The trouble with nearly all writers who oppose birth control is that they consider only proximate instead of ultimate effects. They want large numbers of high quality citizens. Therefore, they contend, let the existing high quality citizens have more children. They assume that families now living in comfortable circumstances will be able to maintain their standards, no matter how many additional children are born. In other words, they expect quality to take care of itself.

We advocates of birth control know that one cannot make quality by insisting on quantity. One cannot make better people simply by having more people.

Mr. Roosevelt says that in order to make a man into a better citizen, we must first have the man. The right environment in which to receive and develop the man is of greater importance. Society, as at present constituted, does not provide the means of rearing unrestricted hordes of human beings into intelligent citizenship. Therefore, birth control has become necessary as a check upon the blind working of ignorance and poverty.

When considering the problems of the class known as the "submerged tenth," even the most conservative are willing to admit its need of birth control. But it is an error to suppose that the proportion of families sunk in destitution constitutes only one-tenth of the population. Figures are available to prove that it is closer to three-tenths, or well over one quarter.[2] The census of 1910 shows that 10.7 per cent of married women in the United States went to work outside their homes to help keep their families together. There, without looking farther, is a submerged tenth among women alone. There is little doubt that the proportion of wage-earning mothers has greatly increased since 1910, and it is equally beyond question that an enormous number of poverty-stricken women are prevented by their excessive family burdens from seeking to earn money outside the home.

They who ban the open and legal dissemination of birth control practically say—Let the slums spawn if

---

1. Editor: Sanger's "voluntary motherhood" was one-sided. It meant that poor women must not to be deprived of birth control. But she also supported what might be called "involuntary non-motherhood." The "existing racial and class conditions" remark hints at coercion, as does the article itself.

2. Editor: Roosevelt distinguished poverty from actual parental inability. Sanger did not.

they must; the prime aim is to goad the upper classes into greater fertility. Both effects are deplorable. There is no greater national waste than the spawning of the slums, with its resultant high maternal and infant mortality rates, child labor and prostitution. As for increasing the fertility of the upper classes, it is certain that the majority of such parents even now have as many children as any rational eugenist could ask them to do, were he in possession of all the facts of each case—health, income, educational needs and provision for the future, etc. Admitting that they give birth to fewer children, the fact is that they bring, relatively, to maturity almost as many as the poor succeed in doing. The following figures prepared by the French authority, Dr. J. Bertillon,[3] demonstrate this point.

For the whole of France 86.6 per cent of the children of rich parents reach twenty years of age, and only 48.6 per cent of the children of poor parents. The figures for Paris give a fertility rate of about 100 births per 1,000 poor mothers, and of about 50 per 1,000 rich mothers. Combining these with the former figures, it appears that for each 1,000 rich mothers there would be 43.3 children surviving to twenty years annually, and for each 1,000 poor mothers only 48.6 children. In France, as elsewhere, the poor mother is handicapped in rearing her surviving offspring. This results in a percentage of unfitness, and the contribution of the high birth rate classes to the adult effective population is consequently no higher proportionately than that of the low birth rate classes.

The world over, the intelligent parents of three children or less have been, and are, the upholders of national standards. This is particularly true of America.

By regarding the bringing of a child into the world as a great social responsibility, the modern American woman shows a fine sense of morality. Since the State does not compel marriage, but leaves it to individual choice, she does not see why motherhood, which is a much more serious problem, should be enforced.

The American woman of today is physically and nervously unable to compete with her grandmother in the matter of bearing unlimited offspring. In Colonial times, the environment was favorable and women specialized on reproduction with eminent success. The prospective mothers of this generation are compelled to divide their creative energies between child bearing and social and economic complexities. It has been estimated that last year seven and a half million women were engaged in industry in the United States, the majority of them in

nerve-racking trades. Ten hours a day at a sewing machine or a telephone switchboard are not conducive to either a physical or mental receptiveness to maternity.

It is a very common fallacy that the decadence of Greece and Rome was due to the artificial limitation of offspring. It is surprising to find a historian like Mr. Roosevelt repeating the error. During the periods he refers to, birth control was, indeed, practised, and as a result some of the greatest poets, thinkers and geniuses, generally, of that, or any other age, were developed. Birth control was one of the few serious moral forces at work tending to preserve the integrity of the State. But, in Rome especially, it was not quite effective enough to combat the soft luxury and vice which had come as an aftermath of an orgy of conquest.

The falling birth rate of college graduates, as demonstrated by the statistics gathered in Harvard and Yale by John C. Phillips,[4] should not be considered alarming. **The best thing that the modern American college does for young men or young women is to make of them highly sensitized individuals, keenly aware of their responsibility to society. They quickly perceive that they have other duties toward the State than procreation of the kind blindly practised by the immigrant from Europe. They cannot be deluded into thinking quantity superior to quality.** But they can be trusted not to suffer extinction. The operation of natural law will prevent the ratio of reproduction from remorselessly falling to zero. In this, as in all other population phenomena, a new level of fertility is being sought—that is all.

MAKING A BAD SITUATION WORSE.

---

3. Editor: Jacque Bertillon (1851–1919), author of *La dépopulation de la France* (1911).

4. Editor: Included in this book as Chapter XVII.

In many other isolated groups, the same process can be observed today. The editor of *The Journal of Heredity* has found that out of 1,512 families of Methodist ministers in America, the average number of children is now only 3.12. The birth rate in the English Society of Friends has fallen from 20 per 1,000 in 1876 to less than 8 per 1,000 in 1915. Or, to take an illustration from an entire racial group, statistics show that the size of Jewish families in Europe has been rapidly decreasing since 1876. They contain now only two to four children, with a growing tendency to restrict the number to two, whilst only twenty years ago they had four to six.

But it is well to emphasize that we advocates of birth control are not so much disturbed by the stationary birth rate of the thinking classes, as by the reckless propagation of the ignorant. We consider that the falling birth rate is a worldwide movement of civilization.

Mr. Roosevelt quotes approvingly the statement of a French newspaper that the present war was really due to the increasing birth rate of Germany and the falling birth rate of France. Had Germany had to face 60,000,000 Frenchmen, instead of 39,000,000, this authority holds, the war would not have taken place. In my opinion, two overpopulated nations would have fought even more readily and long before. The war was due to the overpopulation of Germany and Russia, not to France's stationary population. But once put to the ordeal, the French soldiers, sturdy and highly individualistic because they came from small families, proved at the Battle of the Marne and Verdun the efficacy of birth control, by defeating an enemy mechanically much more formidable than themselves.

On the other hand, the same Germany who had failed against France easily routed the hordes of Russian soldiers, who owed their numbers to an unlimited system of reckless propagation. Germany's birth rate is falling.

In 1860 it was 37.9 per thousand inhabitants and in 1912 only 29.1. It is common knowledge that the economists of Europe do not hope for universal peace until the birth rate of Russia also begins to decline.

The intelligent class, with its acceptance of birth control, holds the same position in American society that France does among the nations of the world.

It is an error to suppose that woman avoids motherhood because she is afraid to die. Rather does she fear to live. She fears a life of poverty and drudgery, weighed down by the horror of unwanted pregnancy and tortured by the inability to rear decently the children she has already brought into the world.

—§§§—

Editor: The verbal duel between President Roosevelt and Sanger continued into 1918. One issue of *Birth Control Review* contained the following remarks about the President. Notice that Sanger chose to mail these mothers an issue of her magazine rather than personally bring them a much-needed quart of milk—even as a rather tasteless 'photo opportunity.'

Editorial Comment—1918

"Editorial Comment," *Birth Control Review* (Feb.–Mar. 1918), 16.

Colonel Roosevelt's race suicide rant was bad enough in times of peace. With the poor paying war prices for the bare necessities of life, it becomes intolerable. But there does not seem to be any way of restraining the self-appointed godfather of the American people. His latest ebullition has been to tour the East Side of New York City and congratulate half-starved mothers of large families on their patriotism, while expressing concern at their inability to buy Grade B milk at 15 cents a quart. The accuracy of newspaper accounts is open to doubt, but a report from the *New York Evening Mail,* which we have before us, rings true to the Rooseveltian psychology. An Italian household of father, mother, and ten children is described as being "a family after the Colonel's own prescription, comfortably fixed with a total income of $27 a week." Twenty-seven dollars for 12 persons. The mockery of it! Of an Irish mother, whose husband had been out of work, but who had recently given birth to her fifth child, Roosevelt burst out with: "Straight United States and no whining! That's the stuff!" This in spite of the fact that the woman had told him that one of her children had been sent to the country, a victim of malnutrition. However, we are doing our little best to counteract the effects of the Ex-President's frivolous and dangerous optimism. He may be interested to know that we have sent a copy of *The Birth Control Review* to every family reported to have been visited by him.

—§§§—

Untangling Tolkien

A Chronology and Commentary
for
The Lord of the Rings

by

Michael W. Perry

Inkling Books   Seattle   2003

Contents

CHAPTER

15

Darkness and War

March 10 through 15, 1419

Dawnless Day through victory at Minas Tirith

W. H. Auden captured one of the most important ideas in *The Lord of the Rings* when he wrote, "Evil, that is, has every advantage but one—it is inferior in imagination. Good can imagine the possibility of becoming evil—hence the refusal of Gandalf and Aragorn to use the Ring—but Evil—defiantly chosen, can no longer imagine anything but itself."

At no point in Tolkien's tale is that idea more critical than at this time. Sauron's imagination will fail on two counts. He fails to imagine that Rohan would value loyalty to Gondor above its own safety, and thus does not anticipate the ride of the Rohirrim. He also fails to imagine that anyone possessing the Ring would choose to enter Mordor to destroy it.

W. H. Auden, "At the End of the Quest, Victory" in *The Tolkien Treasury* ed. Alida Becker (Philadelphia: Running Press, 2000), 48. This book has some excellent articles on Tolkien.

Saturday, March 10, 1419—Darkness Begins

By Tolkien's reckoning, the moon is two days past full today.

Day 1 of 6 with Darkness

Day 170
Moon 99% Illuminated
March 4

Gandalf and Pippin with Faramir

Minas Tirith, Gondor

- Pippin becomes Denethor's squire and learns his duties.
- Gandalf rescues Faramir and his men from five Nazgûl.
- Faramir describes meeting Frodo and Sam.

The Return of the King, Bk. 5, Ch. 4, "The Siege of Gondor."

Line of Stewards

The line of Stewards replaced Gondor's kings after the loss of Eärnur, a king who loved war more than marriage. Without marrying or having a child and heir, Eärnur disappeared into Minas Morgul in 450, after foolishly accepting a challenge to single combat by the Lord of the Nazgûl. Denethor II is the twenty-sixth in the long line of ruling Stewards.

The Return of the King, Bk. 6, Ap. A, I, (iv), "Gondor and the Heirs of Anárion."

Merry with Théoden and the Rohirrim

Day 1 of 6 in the Cavalry Ride to Minas Tirith

Saturday, March 10, 1419—Darkness Begins

The Return of the King, Bk. 5, Ch. 3, "The Muster of Rohan." On horseback, Minas Tirith, is some 400 miles away.

Tolkien seems to have imagined Sauron's darkness as a sort of twilight. Théoden's horsemen could see well enough that traveling by day was preferable to traveling at night (even with the also darkened moon just past full). But the darkness still provided enough cover that their movements could not be easily spotted by Nazgûl spies.

Dunharrow, Edoras and beyond

- Théoden and the Rohirrim leave for Minas Tirith.
- At noon they reach Edoras, eat quickly and depart.
- Merry secretly rides with a knight named Dernhelm.
- That night they camp thirty-six miles from Edoras.

Nazgûl Spies

Here Tolkien illustrates the importance of intelligence gathering in war. When Sauron's Nazgûl saw no evidence the Rohirrim were preparing to ride south, Sauron committed them to the battle for Minas Tirith (note the Nazgûl attack on Faramir on March 13) rather than using them to watch his northern flanks more closely. Sauron also seems to have assumed his allies in the south will be victorious. There too, defeat will come because he lacks intelligence of Aragorn's journey through the Paths of the Dead, something that should have been revealed by the enormous turmoil the Dead created in their wake. In war, Tolkien is saying, knowledge of one's foe often makes the difference between victory and defeat.

Aragorn, Gimli and Legolas with Rangers and the Dead
Day 3 of 8 in Military Campaign

Ringló River

The Return of the King, Bk. 5, Ch. 2, "The Passing of the Grey Company" and Bk. 5, Ch. 9, "The Last Debate." Today they travel 90 miles. Downstream from Calembel, the Ciril joins the Ringló river (a tributary of the Morthond), whose name means "cold flood," probably a reference to icy-cold waters fed by melting snow.

- They rest the night in Calembel on the River Ciril.
- By day, they cross the Ringló River in southern Gondor.

Aragorn's Grand Sweep and Sauron's Darkness

Later, Legolas told Merry and Pippin that he believed the Dead following them gained power because of the darkness that arrives today. Again Tolkien is pointing out that Sauron's darkness failed.

Frodo and Sam with Gollum
Day 5 of 5 to Minas Morgul, Day 5 of 8 to Cirith Ungol

To the Cross-roads

The Two Towers, Bk. 4, Ch. 7, "Journey to the Cross-roads." At this time of year, the sun sets about 6:30.

- Just after midnight, they set out.
- Frodo and Sam rest while Gollum disappears.
- Gollum returns, and they reach the Cross-roads at sunset.

Minas Morgul, Mordor

The Two Towers, Bk. 4, Ch. 8, "The Stairs of Cirith Ungol."

- Gollum leads them east along the road to Minas Morgul.
- At Minas Morgul they watch an army march out.

Shared Sunset, Unshared Moonset

For Merry, this sunset comes at the very end of "The Muster of Rohan" in *The Return of the King,* Bk. 5, Ch. 3. The moonset is near the start of *The Return of the King,* Bk. 5, Ch. 1, "Minas Tirith."

Perhaps to show that the separated Hobbits still live in the same world, on March 10 Tolkien has Pippin (in Minas Tirith) along with Frodo and Sam (at the Cross-roads) catch the same brief but hopeful glimpse of a sunset. For some reason, Tolkien did not have the last of the Hobbits, Merry, share that experience. Hidden beneath the cloak of Dernhelm, Merry rides only into growing darkness as the sun sets on March 10.

UNTANGLING TOLKIEN

The day before, just before dawn on March 9, they appear to share another common experience. Riding with Gandalf for Minas Tirith, Pippin observed a setting of the moon that Tolkien links to Frodo. Unfortunately, Frodo's narrative for Frodo and Sam on that day contains no mention of the moon and the two Hobbits appear to have been aroused by Gollum at sunrise, after the moon had set. Tolkien may have confused March 9 with March 8, when Frodo is awakened as the moon sets to save Gollum from Faramir's guards. We know nothing of what Merry, riding with the Rohirrim, is doing as the moon sets in the early morning hours of March 8.

For more on Tolkien's difficulties with the moon in this section, see "Tolkien's Writing Interrupted" at the end of Chapter 14.

Frodo's March 8 moonset is at the start of *The Two Towers,* Bk. 4, Ch. 6, "The Forbidden Pool." The March 9 sunrise, with no moon mentioned, is a little over halfway through that same chapter. Pippin's setting moon of March 9 is near the start of *The Return of the King,* Bk. 5, Ch. 1, "Minas Tirith."

Sunday, March 11, 1419—On the Stairs

Day 2 of 6 with Darkness

Day 171
Moon 95% Illuminated
March 5

Faramir and Gandalf

Minas Tirith and the ruins of Osgiliath, Gondor

- Denethor forces Faramir to defend the fords at Osgiliath.
- That night a messenger warns that Sauron's forces approach Osgiliath.

A Vindictive Father

Though their personalities differ greatly, almost all the characters Tolkien created who are not allied with Saruman or Sauron have virtues that make them appealing. (Even the gruff and materialistic Dwarves show an impressive loyalty to Bilbo at the Council of Elrond.) Denethor seems to be an exception. Here he pressures his one remaining son to die in battle, and his 'repentance' from that deed only leads him further into evil, as he tries to kill both his son and himself.

The Return of the King, Bk. 5, Ch. 4, "The Siege of Gondor." With its numbers increased by additional troops coming from the south, this is the same Sauron army that Frodo, Sam and Gollum watched leave Minas Morgul the night before. Because of its great size, it moves slowly. Sauron believes he has little to fear.

Merry with Théoden and the Rohirrim

Day 2 of 6 in the Cavalry Ride to Minas Tirith, Location Calculated
To Firienwood on the border between Rohan and Gondor

- The riders may have rested the night in Firienwood.

Calculating the Ride of the Rohirrim

Tolkien left most of the ride of the Rohirrim shrouded in mystery. No text records how far they ride this day or where they rest for the night. Karen Wynn Fonstad estimates that they covered 80 miles and rested in Firienwood, which is near Halifirien, the seventh and last of the beacon hills linking Gondor with Rohan. Firienwood stands on the border between Gondor and Rohan. In draft versions, Tolkien gave other rest stops, but the story changed so greatly that they mean little.

For a summary see *The Return of the King,* Bk. 5, Ch. 3, "The Muster of Rohan."

These calculations of a resting place are from Fonstad's *The Atlas of Middle-earth,* "Pathways." For Tolkien's drafts, see *The War of the Ring,* Pt. 3, Ch. VII, "The Ride of the Rohirrim."

Aragorn, Gimli and Legolas with Rangers and the Dead

Day 4 of 8 in the Military Campaign

www.ingramcontent.com/pod-product-compliance
Lightning Source LLC
LaVergne TN
LVHW081324060426
835511LV00011B/1843